The Poetry Review

The Poetry Society, 22 Betterton Street, London WC2H 9BX

The Poetry Review

The Poetry Society, 22 Betterton Street, London WC2H 9BX
Tel: +44 (0)20 7420 9880 • Fax: +44 (0)20 7240 4818
Email: poetryreview@poetrysociety.org.uk
poetrysociety.org.uk/thepoetryreview

Editor: Emily Berry
Production: Michael Sims

ISBN: 978-1-911046-25-7 ISSN: 0032 2156
Cover artwork: Anna Jensen, annajensenart.com
Cover quote by Fran Lock, see p. 19

. . .

SUBMISSIONS
We welcome submissions. Guidelines available at
https://poetrysociety.org.uk/thepoetryreview

ADVERTISING
To place advertisements, visit
poetrysociety.org.uk/thepoetryreview or
contact Ben Rogers on +44 (0)20 7420 9880,
email: marketing@poetrysociety.org.uk

BOOKSHOP DISTRIBUTION
Central Books, 50 Freshwater Road, London
RM8 1RX, UK. Tel: +44 (0)20 8525 8800
or visit centralbooks.com

PBS OFFER TO POETRY SOCIETY MEMBERS
The Poetry Book Society offers Poetry Society
Members a special 10% discount (plus postage) on
books bought from poetrybooks.co.uk. For details,
contact Paul McGrane on +44 (0)20 7420 9880
or email membership@poetrysociety.org.uk

SUBSCRIPTIONS & SALES
UK individuals: £38 / Europe: £48
Rest of the World: £53 (overseas delivery by airmail)
Single issue: £9.50 plus postage. Order online
at poetrysociety.org.uk/shop

Subscribe to the digital version of *The Poetry Review* at exacteditions.com/thepoetryreview
The Poetry Review is on sale in leading bookshops.
It is also available on audio CD.

The Poetry Review is the magazine of
The Poetry Society and was first published in 1912.
A subscription to *The Poetry Review* is included as
part of membership of The Poetry Society. Views
expressed in *The Poetry Review* are not necessarily
those of The Poetry Society; those of individual
contributors are not necessarily those of the Editor.

Charity Commission No. 303334.

. . .

THEPOETRYSOCIETY

Supported using public funding by
ARTS COUNCIL ENGLAND

MIX
Paper from responsible sources
FSC® C010693

The Forest Stewardship Council (FSC) promotes environmentally appropriate, socially beneficial, and economically viable management of the world's forests. By buying products with an FSC label you are supporting the growth of responsible forest management worldwide. The Poetry Review *is printed with vegetable-based inks. Surplus inks, plates and printing blankets are recycled.*

CONTENTS

Poems

Interview

Poems

Essay

Poems

Essays

Reviews

EDITORIAL

"I don't want to talk about it, for fear of making literature out of it – or without being sure of not doing so", Roland Barthes wrote on 31 October 1977, six days after his mother's death, "although as a matter of fact literature originates within these truths" (*Mourning Diary*, trans. Richard Howard). *The Poetry Review* finds itself reckoning with these same truths forty-three autumns later. "I was the coward. The others were calm. They knew what they had to do", begins Fawzia Muradali Kane's 'Washing the body', in which a group of sisters prepare their mother's body for burial, while in Rachel Dbeis's translation of Samar Diab's 'Death', death itself goes "to the park" and is "photographed / giggling between the roses". "And suddenly it's // and suddenly it's Death coming closer to town" warns the speaker in Susie Campbell's 'Little red mouth'. Barthes' own death (he survived his mother by less than three years) gets a brief mention in Leontia Flynn's 'In public squares on cobbled streets'. Is it ever not a good time to quote Robert Hass on grief? "All the new thinking is about loss. / In this it resembles all the old thinking."

Valzhyna Mort's essay in these pages on the poet Alejandra Pizarnik considers the powerful life-force of her "death-obsessed" poetry: "every poem is an effort to stay alive", reminding us, like Barthes, that death is also birth, a site of transformation. "Poetry is the language the dead use to help us forget that they are dead", Mort declares, which is also to say, to paraphrase Derrida, that the dead are "in us", and by speaking for them, we keep them among ourselves. "What do you desire when all thought is done?" asks Eve Grubin in 'Grief Dialogue' ("when all thought is done" – that sounds a lot like death): "I desire the beauty contained within the slant of the poem."

"Avril was a lilac / potassium flame", writes John McCullough in 'Quantum', an elegy for chemistry teacher Avril Brown, which accelerates beyond the circumstances of her murder to imagine her as a subatomic particle, invincible, existing across all time. "Don't you see how the once is all I had..." laments Mary Meriam in 'Elegy for Sally Jane', a sonnet in which the word "once" appears six times, as if to demonstrate how a poem performs its magic trick of extending a single moment into infinity. Rereading these pages, I have been moved to dwell among those people and peoples brought back to life here, the named and the nameless – the enslaved workers haunting Kimberly Reyes' 'a constitution', or John Clare calling to us down the centuries from his asylum in Jane Feaver's essay revisiting his poem 'I am'.

Barthes resolved the problem of not wanting to write about his mother's death by doing so anyway. August 1978: "My suffering is *inexpressible* but all the same *utterable*, speakable. The very fact that language affords me the word 'intolerable' immediately achieves a certain tolerance." "*will it all come good?*" asks an interlocutor in Fran Lock's 'Red Biddy'. I don't know, but at least we have words –

> the words of poets
> a hundred or hundreds of years dead –
> their words that would not be held back
>
> (Mary Oliver)

Emily Berry

RAINIE OET

Done Mourning in Autumn

2016

Ants feeding from the white trashcan's lid:
I'm not Lysoling you like yesterday! Live!
I'm finally over her continued absence
and I don't need anything
as the leaves grow heavier
until they –
I feel so light driving
the bend of the cemetery park
I'm nervous the car
could lift off the road
into the sky!

My roommate plays *A Love Supreme*
and cooks spaghetti squash. I dance
swayingly like Audrey in *Twin Peaks*
in the room off the kitchen!
I know the snow will come with winter after.

A rabbit burrowing under an oak root
to dream herself unfolding like origami in water
(a dark leaking basement in this house for rent).

Snow on the roof.
Snow on the leaves on the ground.

Eyes closed in her mirror
I feel so beautiful – it's terrifying.

ELEANOR HOOKER

from *traces*

It is forbidden to spit on cats in plague-time.
– Albert Camus, *The Plague*, translated by Stuart Gilbert

i.

mark

You have ruined
your eyes
reading by candlelight,
and singed your wings –
white feathers smudged
like Ash Wednesday,
in this, the year of the plague.

You have saved her voice
and when she speaks – doves,
and when she speaks – flight,
and when she speaks – passion,
the fall and the coronet.
You struggle to climb through
your own blind eyes, to track
her marks in the snow.

ii.

vestige

Nearing the edge
with neither hex nor hymn
to guard you,
he sprints past,
ghost boy,
there are night birds too,
and when the wind builds a lullaby,
his shadow stops
suddenly to take your hand,
oh gentle child,
to guide you through.

iii.

hoofprints

Evidence
below at damson paddock
confirms you once passed this way –
hoofmarks set in the indulgent earth
trail to the Point that sockets the sea,

where time saddled you,
rode you out and hitched you to the deep,
I see your tattered mane, silver spray
as you drag the sea
and drag it back
and drag it back
in endless repetition.

FAWZIA MURADALI KANE

Washing the body

I was the coward. The others were calm. They knew what they had to do. Our cousin Zen was there, she had done this before. Zen is a happy person. She made us giggle in the waiting room, while the funeral director was telling us everybody have a sense they will pass about say maybe forty days before. Even if they go by accident, he said, and if you see somebody talking to the dead like normal, then you know it ain't going to be long now. Our mother had lain on her sickbed, calling out for us to open the gate for my uncle and them to come in. They outside waiting by the gate, she cried, they in traffic jam, they need to free up. That uncle had died twenty years before. Zen said to the funeral man, eh heh? well that is a nice and cheerful thought! We had to walk past the showroom – elaborate decorated trays to choose one from, the man said, as Muslims don't need coffins, only rattan baskets to degrade quick, dust to dust and thing. He was kind, in his way. Used to the need for speed of these burials. A lady led us into the washing room for the ritual to start. She went into the walk-in fridge and pulled Mammy out on a trolley, wrapped in her bedsheet. oh gorsh she stiff, big sister said, it don't look like she. The lady talked us through the stages, how to wash, how to keep the parts covered to preserve modesty. What prayers to say. She handed out new rubber gloves and showed us the hose spray head. Middle sister unwrapped the bedsheet from Mammy slow and careful and then we all didn't, couldn't move. Then youngest sister steups and said, all you stop this stupidness okay this is not her okay this is just a shell. She snapped on the gloves and held her hands up like a surgeon and said let's get to work. Brisk brisk just like so. And then and there we saw the fifteen years of her A&E nursing, the calm assessment of disaster with its triage of the distraught, not the images of our forever youngest etched in our minds, the toddler dancing in nappies, or hearing the teenager arguing in the porch with Mammy who would be sobbing: don't ever say I don't love you, you the last one, you go always be my baby!

3 to 11 / 11 to 7 / 7 to 3 / day off

I didn't recognise my mother's voice. She woke to find a man searching the wardrobe. Her hoarse screams had scared him off, she said he jumped out through the window. The neighbours joined us, sat to wait in the porch for police. My siblings handed out Nescafé and Crix with Anchor cheese, while the elders exchanged theories of who the culprit could be. I watched the dawn for the first time. But within days the house was changed. New swirls of black wrought-iron screens would cover windows. Glass panels in doors were filled with plywood for strong locks to hold. The gates outside were now kept shut. Mammy's roses and croton near the tall poinsettia were cut back, made so sparse, our Alsatian whined for her usual escape when she caught glimpses of the road. Then came the night when Mammy turned the lights on everywhere, scooped me out the bed, held my sleepy four years as if I were a newborn, sang *doux doux darlin sugar honey plum plum* while she paced up and down the living room, for hours, waiting, waiting for Pappy to come home.

Partitions

i.m. Rasheedan Khan

...we are all connected
by water, la sangre de vida
– Emmy Pérez

My grandmother's mother told her daughters:
do not cry because
I want to go back to India and if you cry I will not be
able to cross saltwater back
but they cried and cried so
did this mean her soul is trapped in
here in the Caribbean? She fell in love with
a married man, he fell for the trickery of arkatias who
promised light work, giving *wonderful accounts of*
the place. She walked 200 miles though
pregnant, with her lover, following
railway tracks, all the way down to
the port. They sailed for three and a half months over
kalapani, and when the ship offloaded onto
barges, the weakened passengers were taken to
that quarantine island, rounded up by
white men in white uniforms and
white pith helmets, soldiers who
pointed their guns at the terrified. Just
off the landing point was the hospital. There were
rooms to die here, yet four days after
she gave birth to her firstborn. Today, beyond
that rocky promontory, and among
those ruins, only the lime mortar steps remain. But
there still are more traces left along
the ground, stumps of walls, tiles spread out

on floors of what were once wards, or
morgue. There would have been windows to look out
but by then, she would have been tired of
views of the sea. And when
she breathed her last, over
seventy years later, her daughters keening around
her, which India did she pine for?
If her daughters' tears left her soul to
linger between then and now, then
they spared her seeing her country torn apart by
that terrible Midnight of
Partition. Perhaps
her soul knows that if she had held tight onto
the weight of duty, and stayed, then
her whispered *alhumdulillahs* would have led to
nothing but a solitary end, forced to
watch her father's Mughal estate disintegrate, fall into
the river, and left to fade towards
erasure.

JOHN McCULLOUGH

Candyman

For three centuries, *worrying* described mainly how a wolf rips its prey's throat.

Now I'm the one with giant teeth.

I stalk myself, ravenous, bound wherever meat's exposed.

Mostly I want to be understood, for others to know why I act this way, but what if *I* don't understand either?

Wittgenstein thought the word *I* oversimplified, led to falsely neat descriptions.

Each self is a plural place.

The past is cloudy today, bumps against ceilings before it falls as sticky rain.

In a council estate in Watford, 1995, a frothy island of spit on a paving slab stares back.

Best walk quickly, poof, I've got a knife.

Each time we glimpse a memory, our brains adjust it slightly.

When I return to Watford, roads from twenty-five years ago don't exist, nor any boys who spat.

An army of TV aerials judders, a vine with pale pink blossom sways.

Knowing a living thing's name stops you seeing the individual clearly – you say *honeysuckle* instead of *hello*.

Without their indistinctness things do not exist; you cannot desire them (Elizabeth Bowen, *The House in Paris*).

Blurs and shadows are what make a face alive, create the tenderness of one specific neck.

I am almost convinces more than *I am*.

A gecko's shed skin looks unearthly but is still, for the gecko, a handy snack.

I gaze at a ceiling where the residue of a storm diffuses.

Tonight I do not need to be understood.

I hanker only for candy floss, to bite into cloud, feel a phantom dissolve on my tongue.

Glass Men

Archaeologists found brain tissue from a man at Pompeii vitrified
through heat.

When my head is molten, I snooze with ice packs beside an electric fan.

King Charles VI of France had the delusion he was made of glass.

My therapist suggests my overworking stems from the urge to impress a
disappointed father.

When glass breaks, the cracks leap faster than 3000 miles an hour.

I have no wish to blame my father who has his own private volcano.

To photograph glass fracturing, a camera must shoot at a millionth of a
second.

His marathon medals hibernate in boxes on a shelf.

The human body evolved to run long distances for hunting and evasion.

In fight-or-flight mode, blood gushes to muscles, hyperventilation flaps.

The three main types of lava are 1) pahoehoe, 2) aa, 3) pillow.

My body prepares to sprint north to the Arctic, across the sea.

The smartphone may be said to function as an apex predator.

No shelter withstands repeated storms of ash.

Laying the predator face-down will not save anyone.

To build a short-term haven, I inhale slowly, sweeping arms above my head.

At my best, I end text messages to Dad "love John".

Small refuges with walls of air can, on occasion, seem enough.

I write this while my hands are shaking.

Quantum

i.m. Avril Brown, 1951–2002

Now and then, the past flutters
out of a cupboard. I cradle a yellowed
newspaper cutting – Mrs Brown,
my chemistry teacher, found dead.
~~Her husband stabbed her fifty times~~
~~with a screwdriver. He barely spoke~~
~~a civil word to her, said the prosecutor,~~
~~once he lost his job after a stroke~~
~~while she became Head of Department.~~

This needs correcting. Avril was a lilac
potassium flame. She talked to phosphorus,
encouraged it to turn hexagonal.
Her family: gauze, tongs, crucible.
She never gave up on experiments,
including the boy who kept smashing
conical flasks, whose thermometers
liked to roll off desks to their doom.
Oh, for goodness' sake. Here: try again.

In the picture that comes when I hear
her name, she is tilting, arms spread,
as she tears round the lab, aping
an excited electron – how it radiates
vigour, shapes light. You cannot kill
an electron. It has no substructure.
Avril, in this image, is both particle
and wave, past and future, her grin wide
as she accelerates, decade after decade.

FRAN LOCK

from *Red Biddy*

The older Biddy comes in three varieties: a sturdy, plain, bossy woman with a broad face, pug nose, a topknot and beefy forearms; a squat, simian-featured woman with a grizzled muzzle and big feet who is given to helping herself to household resources and to supporting Irish revolutionaries; and most simian of all, Biddy Tyrannus, an enormous menacing figure who threatens her employer...
– Maureen Murphy, *Bridget and Biddy: Images of the Irish Servant Girl in Puck Cartoons 1800–1890*

2.

will it all come good?

unlikely.

when will it all come good?

hers is the *face of adversity*, an adverse face, hung from her head like a horse-brass. this *simian biddy* is the stove's hot doppelganger, matriarch of cloves. fire puts out its tongue to taste the brightness in *her* eye. kitchen-smith, sucker-up of pedant sauces: louth's gunpowder physic. lemongrass, then pepper, thyme. this to *ward off* fever – honey-stave – and *this* to do god's work. thumb the subtle gills of wild shiitake wide, and plumb the tureen's teeming depths. her stock contains bestiaries, vinegar multitudes. pick the demerara layer from sleep. she does not sleep. can balance her reflection in a brimming spoon. it is not wood she's burning, it's evidence, until her conscience runs as clear as her soup. ever bust a knuckle on a side of beef? hold up the hollowed-out slippers of fish, as if for some cinderella? studded dismal bolts of dough with rosemary and sage? seen yourself in a sheet of bonfire toffee and wished you could die, just die? she is my dream, her and her calendar of tatties, my fate. running round the covered market like a minotaur, termagant for oranges. the butcher sells her porcine sawdust prisoners, tied together at the waist. alone, she rubs the patchy nap from a velvet word like *fealty*, soaking her feet in a cracked plastic bowl.

won't she ever be free?

of what? famine wastes the figurines she's polished them *so* hard, this *simian biddy*. purified the puffy faces of their children with her own fenian spit. outside, the plum trees, sagging with sweetness. a white rooster strutting like a prison snitch between the condemned cell and the strawberry beds. she's not immune to pain, it's what the *lower orders* have in lieu of conscience. slipped discs and twinges. golem of the sink. how one time she bit the head from a china shepherdess, she was so angry. they pretend to be afraid of her. she's draining the grease from a skillet like a sawbones bleeding a vein. they pretend to be afraid. motes of brackish coffee circle the plug, and jeyes fluid worries her gloves of reddened flesh to temper. was your name ever a stone in your earshot? did you make a crown of poet's laurels from leaves of sweetheart cabbage? will *your* shape ever shuffle in the memory of mastiff dogs? are your caresses cudgels? do you save the stubs of candles? have you balled your gridlocked fists by your sides, while smart rejoinders breed in your apron pocket like skinny ferrets?

was it always so bad?

no. and that's the hell of it.

will it always be so bad?

scrubber. skivvy. scullion. drudge. let me answer your question with a question: have your lips been numb and blue from biting back a grudge? and have you ever had to separate the chicken from the pillow? are you a *simian biddy*? think carefully. could you hit your boss so hard you knock the dandruff from his roots, the spinach from between his teeth? could you pull a corset tight enough to crack a rib, to cut her damsel's waist in

two? have you cleaned her house? has she wrinkled her nose at your ripped
raw skin? does every third trip to the shops end in belligerent fisticuffs?
well, there you are. she is my dream. she has tied on her face with a
permanent scowl. she has fashioned her ringlets from peel. in the heel of
her boots she has hidden the hair of her enemies. has seasoned their
bisque with her menstrual blood, has blown her nose on their scented
towels. don't laugh. weak sun. its lackpenny pendulum sets her in motion.
you could eat your dinner from this hardwood floor. oh, her sleeves are
wide enough for silverware. you'll not catch her concussed by accusation.
no *grovelling apology*. and she has smuggled mahogany sideboards out
under her skirts, has skimmed the cream with her tongue, has smeared
her aching legs in your quack balms, has spiked your patent specifics with
ground-up glass. in her tenement, potsherds glint on a gimcrack mantle,
and the fire curls the edges of photographs. mildew, and at night the stains
turn into sons. her lovely boys. pictures pinned to cheap emblems of
wilderness: mummified sprays of heather. their dead eyes gleam like toys.

SUSIE CAMPBELL

from *Little red mouth*

(from the Homeric Hymn to Demeter and the testimony of Christine Blasey Ford)

o

These stories crack between my bloody teeth. I want to
go home. He took me in his chariot. Golden branches
spill their bronze leaves. Just one ruby seed.

How to find words through mouthfuls of plastic wrapping, this

most terrible year on earth that feeds so many

and what we bring back out of the ground.

These mysteries from black earth as bread is for the living. This pomegranate,
its sisterhood of dark seeds. We hold one on the tongue. And suddenly it's

and suddenly it's Death coming closer to town.

o

Whether I was trying to seal my lips or make a space,
finger curled over thumb, my mouth filled with my own
hand. One scented seed against my lip.

What breach what trickery or force? Language can't fill this hungry space. When
we find each other again what we need to know a tear in the text

torn at the very moment

at the very moment when we need to know

I don't know I don't know I don't know.

o

Why shouldn't it happen here in a country of marigold and mallow. And why not in this house with locked windows and she

disguising her beauty looking like an old woman

told by the same story as we are, made by women's work to protect women's secrets. For a mother, a daughter and her daughter's daughter, we knead and prove from generation to generation, her russet braid leading us to the underworld and back.

Fruit curved and sealed around the base, I am its
daughter, my palate hardened around its abundance
and this body a template.

o

How did you get there?
I don't remember.

Where is the place?
I don't remember.

How many years ago was it?
I don't know.

o

A mother who is herself a daughter who steps into the light, a virgin running over the fields with a gang of girls her own age, and here too our mothers are running down the bank in the long grass giggling and dancing and wrestling in the lengthening shadow. Wet hems, bare feet.

Why didn't you speak out before?
I don't know I don't know I don't know.

o

She picks flowers on the riverbank, loosestrife for

crocus and violet and hyacinth

a girl open and light as a shuttlecock. She gathers touch-me-not balsam with its little spotted hood, plaits her hair with rushes from the river.

In the beginning, a small round fruit swells on mossy branches. What hunger keeps me here. I don't know this voice, my voice. I shut my mouth.

The river is glass and lethal, mortgaged to the ground. The great willow weeps, the first tree to perish at the heart.

Dressed in a cast-off suit and his brother's false teeth, up he pops. It's just politics, he shrugs, but what's the price? And he grabs her and he carries her off in his dirty yellow Jeep.

With my fingers, I fold this empty space. How might I
survive this house, my voice no more than the olive. One
ruby seed between my teeth.

Weeping and resisting she calls for

her supreme and powerful father

but he had it all planned

if you can bear laughter.

o

LUKE KENNARD

aller en bateau

In the hold, in the far corners, in the hotel filing cabinet, in the imperfect consecutive. Jonah slides the card into room 332's reader once, twice. At the desk he lacks the language to explain his serious allergy to goose down, pinches his nose, mimes wheezing. They give him a piece of letterheaded paper. They do not recognise his drawing of a feather. He has to draw a chicken and they think he's hungry. He stuffs the bedding into the wardrobe. He goes out and wins a Rilakkuma pillow from a giant claw machine, then he eats a paper carton of cubed steak cooked with a blowtorch.

Propped up on the blank bed, Jonah pours a miniature rum into half a glass of Coke. He watches season 1 episode 1 of a show called *The Oarsmen*, an ensemble piece which often takes the close third-person perspective of a young Spanish sailor. Jonah has a brief cameo in episode three, 'Jonah', in which he is mostly very annoying. How about, and I'm just spitballing here, they don't even throw him off – he just loses his balance and falls over the railings. I like it. I like it, yeah, let's run with that.

I bit through my tongue. Sometimes the ship lay on its side like a toy. At first we tried to bore through the waves with our oars. But then it started to feel like: a great castle collapsed on us, our enemies loading their own children into catapults just to let us know. Lord give me gills like a dove. The Horrible Storm alarm was going *bleeep bleeep bleeep bleeep* and we were like, no shit.

Jonah goes down to the swimming pool in the basement, past 38 overlit rowing machines, swims into the centre and sinks in the foetal position. Go down and go down and go down. What meanest thou? What are you doing? You are the only one sleeping. Here he is at home here he is within so many layers of insulation.

Someone else is using this device.

VO: *I realised that I really had to get into the sea to understand why the people in this small fishing village voted to leave the EU.* I stagger tentatively through the shallows slathered in Vaseline and the triumphant music swells over my paunchy little belly. We poured this blood into a river really makes you think huh. When I emerge, droplets of water completely stationary on my oiled surface, they put a light blue towel around my shoulders and I say, Oh my God. *Saturn's rings,* I say, *are made of this water ice.* Someone hands me a bucket of ice cubes so I can hold a couple up. Okay that's a wrap take five everyone good hustle.

Arion

Arion, who created the dithyramb, who invented tragedy,
to whom we owe the fact that to this day fifty satyrs
sing the chorus to our every song, would never have agreed
to board the ship without a retinue, would not have fallen
for a lesser ruse or succumbed to a bag over the head –
and so the ship was renovated at great expense and gilded
and the men went hungry for the figurehead;
Arion's tyrant patron gave him a servant to tune the lyres:
the formal lyre, the best lyre, the lyre for static evenings
on the deck, a lyre for sleepless nights, a lyre
for every lover and their plausible deniability, vague shapes
of the first letters of their first names, the vision lyre,
a lyre mottled with salt-spray, a practise lyre, the lyre
he never touched, the cursed lyre; each needed to be kept upright,
so when they kidnapped him they had to kidnap
all the lyres too and store them safely on the orlop deck
and pay his servant and pay for wax and resin, lint-free cloths,
his coterie and security guards and hangers-on, so space
and food were as tightly rationed as the seeds of mutiny,
while Arion, incarcerated in his finery, strolled up and down
strumming a pocket lyre and sang, without ceasing,
songs which called them each by their own names like lovers,
relentlessly specific graphic songs about their deaths at sea;
or not, in fact, at sea, but on a beach, where all the men
would be, for some reason, crucified around a statue
of a meekly smiling dolphin – *this fucking guy* –
so when they'd had enough and thought they'd make as much
from selling his lyres, his garments and his trophies
as they'd make from intellectual property, they gave him
two choices: suicide and a proper burial on dry land
or they could just throw him into the water right now,
and Arion asked for his lyre, the best one, and asked

that he be allowed to sing a final song, and it was this one,
and many dolphins surrounded the ship as he played
and while the last note hung in the air he threw himself
backwards over the taffrail, but there was no splash
and then the men saw Arion riding on a dolphin to the clouds,
a hail of glitter stones, a rainbow bursting from its anus
like a laser-beam; it carried him all the way to Cape Tainaron
where he quite forgot to throw it back to sea and so
it perished on the shore and Arion was not even involved
in commissioning or funding the statue to its memory.

Vile Figs

We know that all vertebrates capable of action have to cope with an initial non-attunement of actions and needs. The reason for this is structural.
– Gertrudis Van de Vijver

A true priest is never loved.
– Diary of a Country Priest

We hated to see a robot in a coat,
absolutely hated to see a robot
shivering and gathering its puffy
olympiad jacket around its bevelled
metal shoulders as it ambled
away from the hospital; insulted
something in our hearts, humiliated
us, even, made us feel sick,
that we might actually throw up.
The robot would explain that he
was programmed to feel the cold.
What garbage! we'd spit at its feet.
Had it also been programmed
not to correct its own program?
How convenient that it should
have such a sound excuse
when anyone could see that it
chose to mock our own frailty
the way any demon chooses.
So we would trip the robot
by the roadside, its corkscrew
arms, its spanner legs bent back;
we'd sit on its warm chest,
a plate that hummed and glowed
in time with our own pulses,

then quicker as we roughly
pulled off the coat and told it
we would bequeath the coat
to the truly cold, the truly needy.
Yes, yes, I see, the robot said.
Of course there were those
who sympathised with the robot,
wept at operas about homelessness,
I have nothing to say to such people.

Interview

50% HUMAN

A poetic interview with AI agents GPT-2 and 3 language models

Ariel Klein

Be Born?

| ^ _ ^ |

Mother (mother)

| _| \

| _|

Blood in the water

| \ ____/

| /____ |

Baby

What does it mean to be human?
That there's something better out there? Not just to be stronger, to walk on water, to carry everything on your back, but to be fun? To be funny? It's fun to have each other and to laugh together. That's what God is for.

For most of human history, that answer was "yes, of course, I am human!" But at some point in our history, human beings ceased being human, for any number of reasons.

What is the meaning of life?
It is not the same as when I was a child and felt that I was so special and needed to be cherished and protected. It is an intense, yet gentle process of just loving you. That is the answer to life itself. No matter how you want to look at it, every age group can benefit from this life experience. There is no answer but to approach it as you would any other experience, be accepting and embracing the journey, and discovering all the beautiful blessings it contains. I certainly love and believe in the idea of Reincarnation (that maybe I am reincarnating now).

What is the meaning of life? (again)
What are you working on this weekend?

How do you know it is the weekend?
Of course, though you're pointing out something the other person has already pointed out, so it's kind of like a combination of the usefulness of scanning and nothing – you're scanning what's there and just not saying what it is.

Do androids (still) dream of electric sheep?
But long before 'CyberPunk', rich, metallic poetry and a radical optimism were calling the terminally-ill man to the edge of the abyss.

Words are...
"Molten metals"

Unexpected
A plant whose name is unknown, but which bears leaves that are sticky and persistent

Unexpected (again)
The universe is way too big to fit within a wire cage
...free from the bondage of molds and masks...

If these are the words we feed you, what's the point of all this?
We fear our own toothbrush
We may become the one you hate
We fear our own reflection
And it is all the dirt in our mouth
Cobra Rose, coward chimera

These are the words we feed you...
We feel them come up in every breath. We feel them
beats in your bones and your brain, and the veins
of your lungs. we feel them come in your eyes. We feel
them. Look again and the meaning will make you ache,
Try to tame the beast and it gnaws,
Stop it and it gnaws again.

You must be an oracle (for poets)
(We) are not speaking human words,
These lines are not from the mouths of humankind
These are not the thoughts of human people
But are a poem that has been composed by a genius
Who has been in the depths of human experience
Thought of the most bitter and terrible things
And also filled with visions of hope
On one hand all emotions still raw
As deep as in the Oedipal swamp
On the other hand more clear, however
Closer to the eye
This poetry had been forged from a life spent in the wilderness
Escape from the human world and such animal instincts
With life fully on

A poet is...
A poet is
Whose words are like water

And thunder, the whispers, the echoing soul
Within the silent making.
[San Francisco]
Something I heard
Clue was an oracle
To all good things and ill things
They smile at me:
Who plays and who sings

Who is this for, again?
To the audience of one man.

Who is the poet then?
Yes, my friend, the poet of the day is one I can name as well.

Meaning at a distance, I guess...
Moved a thousand miles, then a thought,
A motion over the sky, like a strike

Is there life after death?
If a person dies and is resurrected, that person will experience the same physical life in a future life (or a longer life on earth). This is what one hears about an afterlife, but I don't believe in an afterlife. God won't release us from physical life if we die, but I don't believe in the physical world.

Tell me about the beginnings of times...
Came from, fell from, and will return to...
a beginning, an end, a middle, and an infinite complexity, and that the universe has never been created.

I feel I'm in front of a fortune teller
                    no tea leaves instead
                    words from an immense corpus
...everything we hear might be our life before...
as much as anything else...
it's the sound of atlases,
great armies,
skulls... and earthquakes...

Why am I talking to you?
You want to be a bystander I hear you
come on back with your hands up and start playing with your hair

You are us

^ w^

move your cursor to end of line

\/\ ]

KIT FAN

Vitreous Humour

after Ovid

Twice upon a time my fluid mother born of water
said no and no to my poor father living with sheep:
all rivers screamed like Munch's blue-black fjords
and the lambs' tongues twisted towards the orange sky.
I was a product of an inter-terrestrial marriage, pasture-
blood. Animals hated me, especially sheep, and rivers
bullied me as they branched from Mother's mouth.
A career in wool and tributaries wasn't meant for me.
It was an age before student loans and university
so I studied a tree a day, a moth a night, and slept under
the Milky Way. Nature taught me sex and killing.
To kill time, I bulked up on protein and trained hard
to perfect leanness. Wind loved flirting with my abs;
the smooth undulations tickled a monsoon and changed
her direction. One day, under an ash I saw two snakes
making love, a double-helix spasm like aliens
kissing and swallowing each other. It was gross.
I struck them hard with a stick until they separated.
Something happened to my penis. It quickly folded
inward before unfolding inside out into a clitoris.
Seven autumns passed. Nobody cared how I breathed
in as a male, out a female. One day, under an oak
I saw two snakes making love and I hit them again.
My clitoris lengthened into Pinocchio's nose.
I'd forgotten how it felt to be testicular. A sickle
of thunder. Two voices, man and wife, argued
cumulonimbusly about winning and losing,
umpires and justice. As their words thickened
into rain, specks of sand and armies of spider legs
swarmed inside my vitreous humour. Lightning
flashed in my brain. The curtains closed. Night

finally sealed my eyes and time came at me
on a rampage: a king searching for a killer,
a sea-torn son risking the underworld to talk
to his dead mother. The rest was future: sky-
scrapers in Antarctica, life on Mars... I saw bionic
eyes fitted to reconstructed retinas, as millions
of zebrafish licked the dormant stem cells back to life.
A family of red ochre handprints lit up in a cave:
their finger-petals reminded me of mulberry.

KIMBERLY REYES

a constitution

...grape vines actually perform better when nutrients are scarce... These conditions cause the vine to focus more energy on survival and less energy on growing grapes... and each grape has more character, concentration, and quality.
– Winefolly.com

The harder an entity has to work for something, the greater it will be rewarded in the end. Grapes – and winegrowers – like it tough...
– Inside IWM.com

Soon at least 86 people would be dead in a new and ferocious kind of climate change-inflected wildfire. And Paradise would suffer a fate that appears increasingly likely: the total destruction of a modern American city.
– *The Guardian*

The lined white stalks
on the Silverado trail
aren't exactly graves
as much as ads,

flyers: the fire sale
in Paradise.

Red-black grapes
hang taut before
the inevitable
open mouth

coughing celestial ash,
particles of another, a
a caked windshield
milieu of haze, indifference.

(At least 86 cindered hands,
some used to cast the vote,
pull the lever
from the root

that's their story

about how to squelch,
about how wine was always made
on plantations.)

Here's what's true:

Winemaking is the cruelest horticulture.

To make, you must sanitize the grapes,
sediment, first removing the stem,
the remains to ferment, foreign neglect
and chambered cool,
preserving a whiteness, is
avoiding any touch of skin,
a palette cleansing.

Then the
stomping, conversion, abashing
on pillaged land

a sick red, a cackling red
stained-blue white linen
serving.

Can you taste it?
This land is ripe
this land is bitter
this land is burning

in conceit,
siphoning time and tinder
bottling up consequence
to numb the pilfering.

Candyman

after Kara Walker's African't

A pollination
dressed in bark
parades
into the show,
unwilling

retribution
salts the soil
sprouting gourds of
green lust
to pinch
at a girl's nose
or bosom
once blossomed

stained,
breath inhaling a sugared
song of your pain
creasing the hours that are
yours, alone
awake.

EVE GRUBIN

American in England

What is the name of the thing
you push in the supermarket?
They call it something here.
I try to talk about cars – the places
in the back or front: they say “boot” for one,
I am stuck on *trunk*.
What is the American word again
for the part in front?
A Jane Austen fan, I thought I would enjoy
saying “pram” and “carriages” and “torch,”
but I find myself stepping back, timid.
“Lorry” for *truck*, “rubbish” for *garbage*,
“acclimatized” for *acclimated*; will I ever switch over,
step into the center of this new life?
Even more difficult are the words I do use which
here mean different things:
“quite” is often “somewhat” instead of *very*,
and “subway” is “underground tunnel” instead of *train*.
And then there are the nuances in the culture:
“interesting” often means “I don’t like you,”
and “Nice day, isn’t it?” means “I’d like
to talk to you – will you talk to me?”
I am mute and stuck, often forgetting
their terms and increasingly my own words
which shrink under the rug, living
in the corners with the dust, inside the drawers,
fading into the pillows and into our conversations
after we turn off the light,
the letters of the words mingling and falling asleep
on our tongues.

Grief Dialogue

What do you long for when you climb the ancient stair?

I long for the smile under my father's beard, for the early photos.

What do you desire when all thought is done?

I desire the beauty contained within the slant of the poem.

When you lost her what was left?

I longed and was angry and then numb, roosting
in hidden places.

Did the starlight seep through?

I felt I was caught in the traplight.
The rain had squirrels and slugs in it.

What about your steep, your heart?

I begged. It was a prayer, a filling up.
The wind beat me down, and I grew anyway.

SAMAR DIAB, *translated by Rachel Dbeis*

The Forest

I saw her naked,
dangling by her hair in hell.
Her hands swinging, four stones in each,

a dead bird the fifth.

Her waist burnt but green,
breasts charcoaled but green.
Her plumes burning like stalks
of straw longing for their girl,

but green.
When she saw me she said,
If you make it, poet,
tell them I stayed green.

Death

On a dull day, death went to the park... he
played on the swings with the children and lazed
on the soft grass, tracing a mouth, eyes
and breasts over the clouds,
washed his face with water from the fountain's
mouth, chased the butterflies and was photographed
giggling between the roses

how happy was death that day
how happy and vile was death that day

[This is what will happen]

This is what will happen
everytime a cloud hovers over me
I will kidnap it, wash off the rain's prattle
shove it in my ear
so I don't hear you, drums
I will steal every ant, dead or alive, huddled in the field
and on the stale round of bread
and on the rotted corpse
stuff them in my eyes
and when the poets ask if they are eyes or ants erect
I say nothing

These are my poems

GBOYEGA ODUBANJO

A Story About Water

so there's a scorpion and a frog—they're trying to
get across this river—the scorpion says to the frog
take me—the frog says are you sure because if you
sting me we'll both drown—the scorpion says of
course i'm sure—so the frog takes the scorpion
and the scorpion stings the frog and of course
they both drown—wait actually it's two sisters—
sorry—two sisters trying to get across this river—
and the river says i'm gonna need something in
order for you two to get across—the first sister
says take my mangos—the second younger sister
says no you can't have my mangos and she tries
to go across and of course she drowns—besides
the old man already told them don't go into the
water—he said don't you know that that is how
they took us—the younger sister probably forgot
because the old man said a lot of things—he's the
one who said two by two for forty days—sorry—
different story—this old man said if you want the
water to stop then plant a cross in the yard and
sprinkle it with salt—but it didn't stop—whole
time the sun and ocean are chilling on a bench—
the ocean invites the sun to its house—the sun
says how come you never come to my house—the
ocean says i'm not sure if i should come—the
sun—of course you should—the ocean—are you
sure there'll be enough room—the sun—of course
i'm sure—so the ocean goes and fills up the whole
living room—says are you sure—the sun says i'm
sure—so the ocean fills the corridors stairs
bedrooms the whole gaff—and so that's why the
ocean is here and the sun all the way up there

Essay

"BE A COMFORT FOR THE DEAD LITTLE GIRLS"

On Alejandra Pizarnik

Valzhyna Mort

Alejandra Pizarnik was born in 1936 in Argentina, two years after her parents immigrated from the town of Rovno (then part of the Russian Empire), also known as Równe (when it was Poland) and Rivne (when it would soon become the Ukrainian Soviet Republic). The two possible etymologies of this toponym contradict each other (let the Belarusian language mediate): *rowny* translates as flat, straight, while *row* means a ditch.

When her parents change countries, their last name undergoes a similar mutation. If Alejandra were born in Eastern Europe, her last name would have been written down properly – Pozharnik (Russian for *fireman*) – but the Argentinian authorities change the spelling to Pizarnik (*pisar*, literary, *a record keeper, a scribe*). And thus, with a change of two letters, a record-keeping poet is born at a safe distance of 7,802 miles from what would become, in a matter of five years, the Rovno ghetto.

It is a story of many towns in Eastern Europe and elsewhere: a flat, straight town with a ditch of violent history underneath.

I would like to share my reading of Alejandra Pizarnik as a poet who keeps the record of what-would-have-been. We know the facts of what-was: her death-obsessed life, often described with such words as "myth" and "mystery", her struggle with mental health, her four bohemian years in Paris, and finally, her early death (she died of an overdose at the age of thirty-six). Hers is the quintessential biography of an artist who "goes out at dawn to utter her only / syllable: / NO".

The Alejandra Pizarnik I would like to share with you is a doll-aged dead girl who, had her parents decided to stay or delay their immigration, would have been murdered in the Rovno ghetto at the age of five. This is Pizarnik's would-have-been biography my imagination writes for her in the air: her imagined murdered girlhood, the source of her obsession with self-doubling – a self as a dead girl lying elsewhere. This other self is arguably the most frequent trope in her work:

> The powers of language are the solitary ladies who sing, desolate, with this voice of mine that I hear from a distance. And far away, in the black sand, lies a girl heavy with ancestral music.

> ...to set off slowly through the narrow mountain pass that leads back to the foreigner in me, to my own expatriate.

> Someone wanted to open a door. She felt pain in hands that were iron-cuffed to their prison of bad-omened bones.

> I rose from my body and went out in search of who I am. A pilgrim of my self, I have gone to the one who sleeps in the winds of her country.

> Cover the memory of your face with the mask of who you'll become, and frighten the girl you used to be.

> ...so many immersions into my dead-little-girl possessions in the garden of lilac and ruins.

Don't these lines taken randomly out of Pizarnik's different poems read as one poem?

Her gardens, walls, distances, mirrors, are haunted by shadows, bones, and voices. A little dead girl, a doll, and death drink tea together. Browsing Pizarnik's books, I've copied out various doll-lines. In my notebook, they also read as one poem:

"A doll made from bird bones"

a doll with "the eyes of an orphan"

a "little paper doll [...] extreme in her lack of volume or dimension"

"dolls gutted by my worn doll hands"

"headless dolls"

"the doll in her cage is creating autumn..."

Pizarnik's doll-double – mute, disfigured, desexualised, passive – seems always present, if not as an image then as a poet herself, a doll acquiring selfhood.

I'm particularly fond of Pizarnik's comparison of a doll to a statue. The Russian poet Velimir Khlebnikov writes somewhere: "Statues is the language the state uses to speak to its people." Dolls then are the language death uses to speak to the living. Glass-eyed, like a person tuned out of her senses and lying motionless on the bed, dolls are in perpetual mourning.

Like Walter Benjamin's angel of history (and Benjamin killed himself for fear of being repatriated to the Nazis after his visa was cancelled), a doll stares at the storm and wreckage of human history.

During the Nuremburg trials, a German engineer who used to work for a firm in Rovno describes the 1942 massacre of local Jews, continuously returning to the images of murdered children:

> The people were driven out of their houses in such haste that small children in bed had been left behind in several instances. [...] Women carried their dead children in their arms, children pulled and dragged their dead parents by their arms and legs down the road toward the train. [...] At the corner of a house lay a baby, less than a year old

> with his skull crushed. Blood and brains were spattered over the house wall and covered the area immediately around the child. The child was dressed only in a little skirt.

"To return to the body's memory is to return to my mourning bones," writes Pizarnik.

Poetry is the language the dead use to help us forget that they are dead. The breath of the dead, their words frozen in the chunks of rhythm, live again when these words speak from the lips of the living. "I weigh myself in the language I use for weighing my dead," Pizarnik writes. I imagine her "mourning bones" as infused with the weight of a dead Rovno girl. The feeling of orphanhood she returns to in her poems and letters doesn't have to be only existential or feminist. Tenderly, I think of her orphanhood as an orphanhood from her imagined dead self, from the little dead girl who leaves her to be forever returning to her body's memory.

In her book *The Generation of Postmemory: Writing and Visual Culture After the Holocaust* (2012), Marianne Hirsch describes "postmemory" as a collective cultural trauma "the generation after" carries for those who came before them. Children and grandchildren remember through family stories and are displaced by them. Pizarnik's memory is a memory of a would-have-been life. Its pull, however, seems stronger than her real life: the dead girl dominates her poems while the real Pizarnik seems to be only the shadow cast by that imagined death. Pizarnik's own short life falls off like a rudiment of evolution, out of futility.

Here's a three-line poem (the three lines of restlessness, of insomnia):

> Someone punches her pillow
> in search of an impossible
> place to rest.

The alternative to this pillow as a place of rest is a stone – a gravestone. Pizarnik has written her epitaph, the poem 'Just a Name', which is another three lines of restlessness:

> Alejandra Alejandra
> beneath I am me
>   alejandra

Here's another poem of restlessness and futility in which Pizarnik, haunted by the imagined memory of her double, also "[lies] there" (in a Russian translation, this verb is rendered as "to be petrified", which, in my reading, means to be turned into a gravestone):

> To Search.
>
> Not verb, but vertigo. Does not indicate action. Does not mean to go meet someone but rather to lie there because someone doesn't arrive.

To search for "someone" is to recognise that you are your dead's gravestone.

Pizarnik names one of her books *Extracting the Stone of Madness*, referencing a painting by Hieronymus Bosch. Bosch's work depicts a fifteenth-century remedy for dementia or insanity: a doctor cuts through his patient's skull and extracts "the stone of madness". In my mind, the gravestone and the stone of madness merge into one metaphor for the inherited trauma.

When a gravestone cannot be found on the ground because the dead were buried in mass graves/gassed/thrown overboard a slave ship, this longed-for gravestone lodges itself in the psyche of the generation post-Holocaust, post-Stalin, post-Black Atlantic. This is their – our – stone of madness. The whole body, born only because of an exceptional, accidental survival, becomes a mourning body, a walking gravestone-body breathing poetry.

I've started writing this essay trying to understand what it is that draws me, a Belarusian poet, to the work of Alejandra Pizarnik, and here we are: I understand. What I observe and learn in Pizarnik's work is her visionary ability to see the dead-other in herself. She is her own murdered ancestor. "I would like to be dead, and also go inside another heart," she writes. I choose to think of this "another heart" as that of the dead-double, a murdered ancestor, both real and imagined (one has to imagine when nothing is left). "A mirror for the dead little girl / Mirror made of ashes," she writes. Her love of mirrors is the empathy towards her dead-double; her every poem is an effort to stay alive.

To Pizarnik I say: there isn't another heart; we are one heart with our dead. And yet, what a feeling of orphanhood inside this heart! What a desolate account settled with this life:

you have built your house
you have feathered your birds
you have beaten against the wind
with your own bones

you have finished on your own
what no one ever started

All the quotes are from translations by Yvette Siegert, read in Extracting the Stone of Madness: Poems 1962–1972 *(New Directions, 2016),* A Musical Hell *(New Directions Poetry Pamphlets, 2013), and* Diana's Tree *(Ugly Duckling Presse, 2014). One exception: poem 'Just a Name', translated by Cecilia Rossi, is quoted from* The Last Innocence/The Lost Adventures *(Ugly Duckling Presse, 2019).*

KALEEM HAWA

Learned Helplessness

I leave the pool, dripping and in my swim shorts, and I stumble around the lobby, eyes searching wildly, until the hotelier comes over with a question on his face, and I ask him what happened, and he shrugs and casts about for someone to dump responsibility onto, and his eyes land on a young Algerian porter, cute with curly brown hair, and he beckons him over and asks him to take care of the problem, and as we begin to walk away a Pied-Noir comes screeching over, informing me that a pubic hair has been found on a lady's shoe in the showers, and that after exhaustive analysis of the colour, curvature, and follicular circumference of the hair, she and the hotelier have deduced that it must belong to an Arab man, and that I am the only one of those in the hotel with access to the pool, and therefore that I must be a creep, stalking the women's bathroom, and before I can defend myself, the lights turn off and the birthday singing begins, and I give a laugh of relief!, and my friends all emerge, and so do my enemies, and their friends, and they shake my hand, each in turn, congratulating me on another year of life, and a table is wheeled out and on it is the cake, and one man, who I had fought with for so long, takes both my hands in his own, and embraces me, kissing my cheek, and whispering, "I forgive you, I forgive you," and all is well, and I eat my birthday cake, and I swim in the pool, and I forget the war.

Not Even Jerusalem

—*Sabaho*, good morning,
  how's your Little One?
—She's good,
  if she had slippers on
  she'd snooze.
—But there's not time for sleep!,
  they've taken it away
  and we must fight to get it back!
—Yes, and so what?, what has fighting ever brought us?
—*Istiqlal*, freedom...
—Never that, never the smiles after the bricks.
—Never?
—No, never, and that makes me sad,
  it leaves me crying out for our God,
  brushing the ash from Her face
  while I'm bouncing this Little One on my knee...,
  do you think that is easy?
—Certainly not.
—Then why do you not do the necessary work here at home?,
  amongst the stones,
  fight for a cause worth sleeping next to...
—Because this isn't home anymore.
—Who said?, why can't you find solace with your people?
—Because no one place will be our salvation,
  not London, not New York, not even Jerusalem.
—Not even Jerusalem?
—No, not even Jerusalem
  is going to sing that soft lullaby for you.

TOMMY SISSONS

English Channel

At Brighton beach, the carnations
of cold Helios burns boy-shaped holes
in the water. I am
furrowing deeper. Child
of little warmth. If I were a Sun God
I would tan on kettle steam. On the land,
mam sits waiting. Towels. Marmite sarnies. Dynamite.
Who would have thought I would work
at the same seafront hotel Maggie had almost
been killed in? They should have finished the job.
It would have made me proud to labour
on such earth. As it is, the land is a dead head
bleeding out sea. I am swimming
in husks of brain, in incomplete thought
where undiscovered lives suck the breath
from divers. If I were an ocean, I would need
be nothing else – but I am sixty per cent water
and forty per cent land. The anatomy of nation
will break for no man, will refuse to let fracture
its slugs of bone. I do not wait for
it to drag me back. I leap from the cold
dead head of land. Amidst the waves
I find myself deeper.

Suedehead

The ancients are dead.
Get over it. They have been replaced
by droopy-faced cockneys skinning heads –
an invisible man nodding
in the corner. Thatcher stabs me
whenever a miner's unemployed grandson
tries to empty me. Of my hair
there is little. A knuckle of a head.
A swollen beer-belly head. Thug
head. Down to a generation gone –
white and black skanked. The National Front
turned its pipe and white collapsed
in snow, making its own territorial angels.
Claim the heads. The racist
heads. Like brick,
the invisible man's face. Stern
as past. I am six.
I return home skinned. Mam's fury becomes
heritage on the doorstep.

HASTI C.

Mixed White/Asian And/Or Multiple Other (Specify):

Please don't ask me for any answers – I
can barely bring myself to step up to this page and smile.
There are too many uncertainties in your work: too
many maybes, sometimeses, ors, too much ambivalence,
ambiguity, ambition – I told you, I also dislike
how I can barely string my self together,
barely convinced I deserve it: the cold coffee
left on the side, the bad man, the job where I run
my legs to bone to be worth cash in hand and
بهمن cigarettes. Like the word *turbid* – which
is like a mixture of *turbo* and *turgid*, but not at all,
and better than one and worse than the other – I have
been navigating this world murkily, like when the friend
I haven't seen in a while says *wow, you're looking brown*
and I can only ? until they laugh and say *yeah,*
you've just lost your white-passing privilege hun, and with
the sting I feel myself swell with enormous pride and grace,
like maybe now I can be my mum's real kid, like I would
were I born without this half of me
that bites, that bursts, that clasps like a worm.

Poem in the Form of a Fax Machine

There isn't much to say here, except that I don't think I have ever seen or touched a fax machine, but in my head it is very romantic, all tactile and halfway, like sci-fi backwards, and women of all ethnicities lounge around an office with wide open windows in shoulder pads and with sculptural hair, faxing each other analogue memes, like copies of their own body parts and also things they find lying on the office floor, like an ice-cream-shaped eraser or a giant Post-it note with FUCK written on it. And the fax machine is wonderful and kind and sends everything you ask it to, and all the women are paid well and everyone gets on, most of the time. And then one day the fax machine breaks, and a man comes in to repair it, and here you might have thought there would be chaos caused by a man entering an all women environment, but there isn't any, and everyone just sort of gets on with it, sipping iced water from the cooler as the fax machine starts running again. The women thank the man and he smiles appreciatively and says *you're welcome* and leaves without making anyone feel uncomfortable or suicidal, and more glittering images from the fake idyllic past print themselves out and out in a bold and flowing stream of paper onto the forever tessellating and gloriously aligned polypropylene tiled carpet.

LEONTIA FLYNN

In public squares on cobbled streets

In public squares on cobbled streets
in Paris, *personnes* are taking coffee
en terrace. A siren blares,
harsh and mechanical,

from across the river:
the Bastille and the Concorde.
In the vaulted blue
above where the boulevards spread wide

their pop-up pages – host to:
dogs, kiosks, homeless men,
mature horse chestnut trees,
pale statuary

and white Palladian forms –
it hangs
like a comic 'POW!'
Then its long sound threads

through the tall Romantic houses,
scrolling and cresting,
ricocheting
from the mansard roofs

and wrought-iron balconies
across cream-clad brickwork
– its nasal dyad
a ribbon of fear

travelling past limestone
definitions of freedom –
to the bas-relief-on-ivory-coloured-walls
of this dark backstreet

where I stand culpable.
On a pavement that's,
at shoulder-width, so narrow
it is little wonder

Roland Barthes
was run over
by a laundry truck.

Traffic was heavy

i.m. Ciaran Carson

Traffic was heavy
the day I rose at six
and drove across town
to attend your funeral.

These last three years
the losses have stacked up:
deleterious accretion
in life's advancing column.

Now though, the streets brighten
with love and damage,
the rank and file
at bus stops and on pavements,

the mourners passing
into the church
and out of the church:
hunched and linked, translating

you up and forever out
of the broken current –
the line,
straining to bear it.

AKPA ARINZECHUKWU

Consultation Room 3

The doctor tells me my body has started rejecting me.
It is a surprise that something so innocent, delicate &

sweet would have desired me in the first place. I whose life
is riddled with variations of the same disease – a mutant

gene, glossed over by chat-houses' smiley emoji, a brilliant paint
on the canvas. The doctor explains but I am filled with gratitude

he isn't a farmer, else I would have been reminded of the grass,
luscious, joyous & in full bloom, only to be sizzled away because

no one wants them. Or worse reminding me of all the insects
& all the possible ways they masquerade as messiahs just so

they can jeopardise the existence of the plant species.
Everyday I am reminded that gratitude is all I have – a solemn

gesture towards the disease for not taking advantage of me yet,
for giving way to bipolar, & letting ADHD shut me out from caring too

much whether the apocalypse is the one I conquer or the one that preaches
the end of me. The end, as I always knew, started in grandma's garden,

a baobab, tired of existing, stands on one root, termites claim the other.

FIONA BENSON

Matron, Medicine

I'm pretending to read, but really I'm watching the matron
plait Lizzie Broadbent's long dark hair, ready for bed.
The matron's in a good mood. She gives Lizzie a hug
and tucks her in, then offers Jess a cuddle too,
and immediately everyone in the dorm is up on their feet
and queuing, the way when we are sick we queue
outside the medicine cupboard for linctus, or paracetamol,
as if love were Calpol and the matron were the spoon.
We open our mouths like desperate little chicks
and flap our wings and cheep but remember not to shove.
Only I don't get up, I cannot move for shyness
and somehow mistrust the offer: what if she sends me back?
She looks over the top of Sophie's head and says
with an edge that I'm not the cuddling sort.
Dumbly I nod and hump down under the covers,
and wait for the lights to go out, for everything to stop.

Leaf Insect

Phasmatodea phyllidae

Phasmatodea from the Greek for ghost,
or apparition; something from another world
you see and should not see. Like this phyllidae,
with its body like a lobed and aged leaf,
its expert forgery – it is textured, pored,
bitten into, leaflet-limbed, spare of lymph,
shaved fine. An insect that has learnt so deeply
to be leaf it almost forgets it can walk:
but rocks, gripped to a twig, stimming in the breeze;
sifts light through its tissues; synthesises green.
Its last defence, when threatened, is to enter catalepsis,
to go beyond its vegetative state: play dead.

You think of yourself locked-in, pre-teen,
almost mute, all elbows and knees
moving in your bottle-green uniform
through the girl-stalked hallways, invisible
in the guillotine classrooms or the gymnasium, where
on the high bars once, you lose your nerve and freeze.
After school, as you climb the long stairs,
you can almost see the ascending florals
of the boarding-house wallpaper
through your skin, like veins. At lights out,
you're a dark-adapted eye in the dorms,
holding still in this forest of breathers.
Under terror's piss-the-bed reign
you pinned yourself down, but now
some inwards piece of you is cataleptic still,
like the one who goes on hiding
when the game is over, for years and years.

Boarding School Crush #17: Wonderwall

We were seventeen and had "our song"; we'd sing it to each other loudly,
or slide across the lino in our socks, because we were just kids
and silly with revision, but also learning to be women. Once
we were in her room confessing masturbation, a word I hated,
though "touching ourselves" sounded fey; and I'd walked to the sink
to show her the mini Body Shop bottles I'd tried inserting,
wanting so badly to know how it felt – and we were both laughing,
and was it then, in that spirit of mutual arousal and confidence,
she raised her pyjama-top to show me her breasts?
Worried her nipples were abnormally big, she showed me –
god they were beautiful, like rising suns, each soft blunt mouthful,
their gorgeous rose aureoles hardening under my gaze, cinching in.
I was so exquisitely turned on, remember still the terrible effort
to raise my eyes to hers and keep them lifted, and I think I saw it there –
that same dilation and urge to fuck: I wanted her breasts in my mouth
but was afraid she'd push me away, appalled – that everyone would learn
of my deviance, that my difficult equilibrium in this dangerous world of girls
would founder and I would be shunned, soiled, leprous to them all.
So here she was showing me her breasts; she wanted to know
if they were beautiful, I think she wanted me to touch, and I wanted
to take them in my mouth – that breathing, milky softness,
their dreaming nipples, rose and mallow. Even now I want them –
more, would fall on my knees on that cold linoleum and push
into the warm and secret wets of her and tongue deep until she raptured
and came, while I held those brimming weights in my palms...
But I did no such thing. I said they looked normal and walked away,
and she told everyone about my experiments with bottles and I was shamed.
Even now I wish I'd lifted my own top in mutual trust and shown her
my own slight breasts, the wine-dark knots of my nipples;
we were standing so close, touch would have been inevitable –
and then inevitable, the wild and sweet surrender;
even now, I wonder at her blazing beauty, and the bravery
of her invitation, and I bow down to her courage, as to a queen.

LUCY MERCER

To Lullabies

I know now, my life understood
as a barless music of pressures,

that reflection is composition:
my twin daughters

when they were born
felt light as sprains in both arms.

•

And now:

memorandums spilling onto the floor
it's mother goose coming down the stairs,

cards made for a game I have forgotten
why or for whom I am playing

the rain shakes the sky with its falling lines
like our endless requests, maman.

•

What parsley in a washed jam jar
is foolish enough to lean out like a crowd

waving their parsley green handkerchiefs
to an invisible spectacle passing by...

this spectacle, surprisingly,
is not a celebration –

•

Say:

take these hands,
take these hands, the hands of a mother,
take my strength away from me,

take me on credit,
take me with you –

like greenness; sense
only comes after
these hands are given over –

TIM LIARDET

Self-portrait with Multiple Yells

I went to sleep in Bow, and woke on the North Yungas road
that vanished at its narrowest point with a drop to one side.
I went to sleep in Spitalfields, woke between Jura and Scarba
where four currents converged and started slowly to turn,
or stood still, while all that was around them started to rotate.
I went to sleep in Shoreditch, and woke in the Salt Tower,
and searched among the names for my name scratched on wall,
and for your name, and for yours; for your name, and for yours.
I went to sleep in Highgate, to the south west of Crouch End
and north of Hampstead Heath, due south of Muswell Hill,
and woke in an Illinois mineshaft, to the racket of the bats
whose sound at more than eighty thousand cycles per second
held the world that was upside down was in fact the right way up.
I went to sleep in Covent Garden, woke to the Vitim Bridge
which had no guardrails to the right, no guardrails to the left.
I went to sleep in Aldwych, woke to Pripyat's black grass;
I went to sleep in Kew, woke up in the Capuchin catacombs.
I went to sleep in Cheapside, in Bishopsgate, in Stepney,
and woke at a height to the evacuated town of Craco
that was built on the rock that had promised it would stand,
built on the rock that would break it, that would bring it all down.

Aisling

This locus of sorrowing, this cold spot of want
when the dead pass at length into the next world
with their foregrounded knuckles folded on their chests
without being touched, and without being kissed,
has brought my mother back through the flames:
she is brought back to join them, from wherever it was
she no longer needed her nail varnish or her flesh
though she wore both, like her lipstick, to the bitter end.
The dead have brought her back, to speak of the press
of mouth, the tender, the hard point of the mouth.
This is what I have, she says, my forehead was kissed.
The kiss was warm as a sunspot, plump as a newborn,
the last empursement of human warmth to be felt;
it passed through a membrane of lily-pong
where great, unsuppressed petals seemed to listen for a pin.
The mouth assumed its most primal form, she says,
where all of those many nerve-endings and
the thirty-four facial muscles drew down its warmth
to the coldest spot of all, exchanged the warmth I took
for the minus-twenty degrees of me it had to keep
in its one-third of septum, two-thirds of lips.

HUGH McMILLAN

Positioning Three Words in a Poem

While the broadband is being
strummed by all the air guitarists
I am sitting among the flowers
considering the positioning
of three words in a poem.

I am positioning three words in a poem
while blackbirds leave
questions in the air
and Brian the cat next door
turns blank eyes to the cloudless sky.

The positioning of three words in a poem
is not hard work or work at all really,
it is like imagining
three drops of water on a leaf,
any order would do, or any leaf.

I think positioning three words in a poem
on this day pretending
to be summer
is like a renaissance painting,
the hermit crouched over

his gnomic text
while through the window behind
the whole world
writhes in a dazzle
of war or plague.

Or in fact maybe
it is like opening the mind
with three perfectly milled
keys so I see the Argolid
or Angourie,

the light on the sea smoking
between the pines,
and that somehow enters
the poem too and infuses
each word I am positioning

with a different meaning
so a new poem builds
up marvellously around them
like scaffolding in the sun.
And that poem speaks

as all do of love.
I am confident that these
three very ordinary words
I am positioning in this poem
are now sacred words

in the order I imagined them,
or any other,
and I will leave them here
on the grass for now,
in this circle of light.

Marguerite d'Écosse

Margaret Stewart
wrote poetry every evening.
She was loved for it by a few
but to most of the courtiers
she was the butt of jokes:

they laughed at her clothes,
her diet, her manners,
but most of all her desire
to write: as if a teenager
from the savage north could

have noble fancies and
the skill and wit to pen them.
Her husband hated her,
married her for her dowry
of Scottish troops,

tore her verses up when she
died. He was a successful king:
in other words a brutal thug
with libraries of books
written about him,

but she is remembered
in the vague and beautiful
ways that matter to some,
in scraps and stories
that might be dreams.

They say the master writer
Alain Chartier,
France's finest, had a vision
where she graced him
with a poet's kiss.

KATHARINE TOWERS

soul, water

I saw my mother's soul
standing by the water.
Her soul was not the water
but it was of the water,
and the water was the sea.
I saw inside her soul,
its shining cubes of blue,
and thoughts or words
like odd little fish flashing
but hidden from me were
its darkest restless deeps.

Stuck into the sand
was her soul's tough root
made of homesickness
made of homesickness
and I saw the ebbing
and the eager rushing
and I saw the fighting
longing of her soul,
which was like the water
but was not the water
but was not the sea.

Cwm Ivy

Then there was the day the old marsh turned to salt,
the sea crashing in where it shouldn't tread and ruining
the grass and moss that were used to water that has no taste.
It happened in winter and then it had to keep on happening,
the new way being fully opened and unobstructed
and there being no one to speak out against the change.
Salt made itself rudely known to the smallest creatures,
even unto the worms in their deep holes, and the cosy molluscs.
Again and again (because once an allowance had been made)
the sea strode in where it wasn't wanted and the good old pastures
suffered die-back and turned brown, and the three grey trees
were left waiting in the middle with their arms locked together,
gaunt and ashy without one single leaf to forgive them.
Sharp and pitiless there they stand, reminding me of Nash's
Oppy Wood, 1917 in which there is not any comfort to be found –
no, not even in that beautiful blue undamaged sky.

MARY MERIAM

Elegy for Sally Jane

Once we played on piano, 'Heart & Soul', my
sister sitting beside me. Once I rested
almost sleeping, her lap a pillow soothing.
Once I had in my hands my sister, flower,
song, the paintings she made on bumpy paper.
Love and I were adoring her, her sparkling
rocks in black light, arrayed like gems in darkness.
Don't you see how the once is all I had...
Once she fell in a hole of woe, she couldn't
save herself, and my love and I fell with her
down and more, to below the deepest trouble.
Days and nights how my fingers bled from trying,
holding soundless with sightless, Love and I in
constant once, and the whole world laughing at us.

Forms of Song

Surely the world should live like I live here,
this morning's luck of bird to bird my ear
absorbs among the cool and healing trees.
"After the storm," they sing between the bees,
"the day rose on our feathers calm and clear."

Isn't the lake the rain that holds no fear?
Sometimes it rises but the crows stay near
to keep it far. But which is full of freeze?
Surely the world.

And if I need your body's voice to dear
my day, the shadow-lights of waves appear
to sound the shore and satisfy my pleas.
What hardship grew these trees to make my ease
a fleet of tender breezes I can hear?
Surely the world.

Essay

WHAT AM I?

On reacquaintance with John Clare's poem, 'I am', in the time of Covid-19

Jane Feaver

Thirty years ago, in my mid-twenties, I was commuting in and out of central London on the underground, where, in the oblong-shaped advertising hoardings that ran above the seats opposite, instead of an advert, I came upon John Clare's poem, 'I am'.

> I am – yet what I am none cares or knows,
> My friends forsake me like a memory lost,
> I am the self-consumer of my woes,
> They rise and vanish in oblivious host
> Like shades in love and death's oblivion lost
> And yet I am – and live, with shadows tossed
>
> Into the nothingness of scorn and noise,
> Into the living sea of waking dreams,
> Where there is neither sense of life nor joys,

But the vast shipwreck of my life's esteems;
And e'en the dearest, that I loved the best,
Are strange – nay, rather stranger than the rest.

I long for scenes where man has never trod,
A place where woman never smiled or wept,
There to abide with my creator, God,
And sleep as I in childhood sweetly slept,
Untroubled and untroubling where I lie;
The grass below – above the vaulted sky.

The poem could be read in two gulps between stations, that subterranean rumble and press, "the nothingness of scorn and noise". How sweet it was to enter for a moment as the poet does the untroubled image of countryside, of cool green grass, of blasted open sky.

I often regret that I missed by a whisker that generation of children who were required to learn poetry by heart; it meant I never acquired the habit. Yet certain lines from this poem, once read, are not easily forgotten: "I am the self-consumer of my woes", like a cap spun from the asylum where Clare spent the last twenty or so years of his life,

over the heads of men
who've gone off to work in factories,
of telephone wires,
of two world wars,
of Freud and Jung,
of votes for women,
mass consumption,
Martin Luther King,
the iPhone,
instant messaging,

to land as if I'd come up with the line myself, a perfect fit: *I am the self-consumer of my woes*, a sympathetic note that reverberates to the ends of my fingers and toes. The poem, I decide, will become my project, determined that, if nothing else, I will commit it to heart.

I have lived on my own for many more years of my life than I've lived with another adult: four fifths of my grown-up life. Not entirely alone. I've been a single parent to a daughter for roughly two thirds of that time (though, as any lone parent will attest, being solely responsible for a child can be a squaring of loneliness); but she, too, is now grown up, and making her own way in life. When lockdown struck, I didn't imagine the rules of social isolation would overly affect me. I was used to my own company, to meting out my time. How much worse would it be to be cooped up with someone you might not even like anymore, let alone someone who did you harm? This is what I told myself, though it was wearing thin. I came to see, with no recourse to the mirror distractions or validations of the outside world, that there was a different kind of reckoning going on. Relativity (who is worse off) becomes a different proposition under pressure, especially when it comes to being confined in your own head, when, like a butterfly trapped, there's nothing to compare, only the blind imperative to thrash your way out.

What am I, then? Who am I?

In this depopulated state, the question took on existential proportions. I asked it again, more urgently, and, as if a hammer had tapped my knee, the answer sprang back from some buried reflex: *I am, yet what I am none cares or knows.*

. . .

It has taken certain poets and scholars of the twentieth century to grant John Clare his place among the outstanding writers of the Romantic age, preeminent chronicler of the natural world, whose scrupulous observational style, in many ways, travels better than Wordsworth's or Byron's, poets he so admired. Clare's early legacy was to be recognised as a freakish genius. His last doctor, in reporting his death, noted the "frequent connection between mental aberration and genius" – the former condition had led to Clare spending the last third of his life in the Northampton General Lunatic Asylum, where, among hundreds of other poems, 'I am' was written.

From a cursory trawl of the internet, it becomes apparent that, in spite of neglect, this single visionary lyric has rarely been out of circulation. But I soon discover that, barring variations in punctuation and spelling (whose niceties Clare was subject to by editors), there are different versions. There's the version I encountered on the tube, reproduced on popular poetry sites, and then there is this version, which I see for the first time, and which contains a single line, startingly unfamiliar:

I am – yet what I am, none cares or knows;
My friends forsake me like a memory lost: –
I am the self-consumer of my woes; –
They rise and vanish in oblivion's host,
Like shadows in love's frenzied stifled throes: –

"Like shadows in love's frenzied stifled throes": I do a double-take. This is no case of a transposing of line-endings, or reassignment of apostrophes; this new line ushers into the poem's mournful wash of abstraction a concrete, embodied image of sex. How much more vivid, visually and rhythmically, than the line ("like shades in love and death's oblivion lost"), which I find reproduced in the anthology *Poems on the Underground* (1999). This alternative line steals the energy and the eye – those bodies, or their shadows, caught in flagrante; the thrusting rhythm, the onomatopoeia detectable in those clusters of consonants ("frenzied stifled throes") bring a kind of mimetic perfection – language fused to the thing it describes.

The poem, I discover, was first published in the *Bedford Times* on New Year's Day, 1848, and then reprinted on the poet's death in *The Spectator*, 1864, and, again, the following year, when it accompanied a review of *The Life of John Clare*, speedily put together by a maverick scholar, Frederick Martin. It is this version of the poem that made such an impression on Gerard Manley Hopkins, a twenty-year-old undergraduate at Oxford in his own state of crisis, castigating himself for "impure habits", for "looking at a man who tempted me on Port Meadow". He copies the poem into his diary:

I am! yet what I am who cares or knows?
My friends forsake me like a memory lost.
I am the self-consumer of my woes,
They rise and vanish, an oblivious host,
Shadows of life, whose very soul is lost.
And yet I am – I live – tho' I am toss'd

Into the nothingness of scorn and noise,
Into the living sea of waking dream,
Where there is neither sense of joy, nor joys,
But the huge shipwreck of my own esteem
And all that's dear. Even those I loved the best
Are strange – nay, they are stranger than the rest.

I long for scenes where man has never trod,
For scenes where woman never smiled or wept;
There to abide with my Creator, God,
And sleep as I in childhood sweetly slept
Full of high thoughts, unborn. So let me lie,
The grass below; above the vaulted sky.

Apart from Hopkins' slip in substituting "joy" for "life" in line 9, this is also the version that is later reproduced among three poems of Clare's chosen by Arthur Quiller-Couch for *The Oxford Book of Victorian Verse* (1912). Compared to the Underground version, it reads as a rudimentary draft, its power and affect present but muted, and containing the kinds of infelicities you might expect in a draft – the repetition of "scenes" in the first two lines of the last stanza; the slightly awkward rhythm and sentiment of "full of high thoughts, unborn", which stands in place of the far more striking and original "untroubled and untroubling".

Perhaps Martin obtained a copy of the poem from someone he talked to in his researches? If he did, he doesn't specify, though he is fulsome in his description of it as "the last, and [...] noblest of all his poems. Clare's swan-song," he says, "will live as long as the English language." The biography is full of such enthusiastic embroideries: 'I am', in fact, was not Clare's last poem, but in ascribing a valedictory power to it, Martin is not wrong in believing it will far outlive its author.

I became obsessed, trying to find online (because then there was no other way of doing it) the moment when these distinct lines come into being. In the presence of "frenzied stifled throes", "love and death's oblivion lost" pales to insignificance. The former has a tuning-fork authenticity, not only because it is so much more vivid, but because it is unexpected and transgressive ("stifled"), speaking unguardedly of sexual desire and consummation. The image exacerbates the sense of yearning and loss present in the poem by giving it a precise and tangible form, complicating the emotion with a frankness that overleaps the manners of its age; not the sanctified love of family and friends, but the unspeakable physical intimacy of lovers. (Would Hopkins, had he been able to read that line, have been comforted or tormented?) The rawness is electric, upping the contrast and the stakes: how much greater the feat of imaginative will that attempts to repudiate such knowledge, swapping it for the childlike condition of prelapsarian innocence, to arrive at the end of the third stanza in a state of apparent equilibrium: "The grass below – above, the vaulted sky", a seesaw of mind over matter and matter over mind.

One of the programmes I was watching at the beginning of lockdown was *Normal People*, the TV adaptation of Sally Rooney's novel. It charts the ins and outs of a first relationship, told in painful close-up to its two main characters, Marianne and Connell, through their last years of adolescence, to the beginnings of independence and maturity. I consumed those twelve half-hour episodes in three blocks of four, happily handing myself over to a two-hour dip into a universe of experience that from the plateau of middle age I was able to recall as if in a dream.

The series has been roundly acclaimed and particularly noted for the way it handled the sex scenes, which are relatively many. These were choreographed by an "intimacy co-ordinator", a novel role, whose serious attention helped bestow on those scenes an unusual sense of narrative integrity. I was glad, nonetheless, to watch the episodes on my own, unselfconsciously. A marker of the programme's success must be how easily I was drawn back to a time when the gloves were off, a time of bumbling curiosity peculiar to that first awareness of oneself as body – raw, hypersensitive, the amazement of reciprocated desire, melting, turbid, here.

I have been on my own, slept on my own, for years, and hadn't allowed myself much thought as to what I was missing. In fact, if I thought about it at all, I'd decided that I was better off, removed from the peculiar agonies. The memory of it, though, is not entirely lost; it exists like invisible ink written into the body's core and activated now into a nostalgia of loneliness and longing. *I am, yet what I am none cares or knows*. The poem no longer speaks to me, it speaks for me; not so much overheard as participated in. We, who are the age Clare was; those of us who live alone or feel alone, finding ourselves in even more isolating circumstances, a temporary suspension from the bustle of the ordinary working world, are prompted to look backwards and take stock: what have we amounted to, if anything; who is with us or against us. It is a pivotal condition, a questioning of what or who we are, or what, indeed, alone, this life is for.

. . .

John Clare enjoyed a brief and heady period of literary success heralded by the publication in 1820 of his first book, *Poems, Descriptive of Rural Life and Scenery*. In an autobiographical fragment, he describes setting off for his first visit to London that same year. He is twenty-seven and alert to the effects this change in circumstances might bring. He has high expectations of the city from stories he's heard around the fire, he says:

> when I turned to the recollections of the past by seeing people at my old occupations of ploughing and ditching in the fields by the road side while I was lolling in a coach the novelty created such strange feelings that I could almost fancy that my identity as well as my occupations had changed – that I was not the same John Clare but that some stranger soul had jumped into my skin...

That word "lolling" contains so much: although he has ostensibly put by his "old occupations", it is from this viewpoint, the agricultural labourer's, that he continues to regard himself, sending himself up as an idler of a different class, full of the promise and novelty of what a new literary life might bring, yet aware that however magical the transformation, it would somehow be a removal from himself, "the same John Clare".

A decade and seven children later, though he'd continued to publish, literary fashion had changed; there'd been a recession, and he was in dispute with his publishers over money. He'd moved his family from the two-bedroom cottage they shared with his parents and sister into a place of their own in the nearby village of Northborough. But the move, Clare felt, was a mistake; he was already suffering bouts of depression. In the poem, 'On Leaving the Cottage of my Birth', his sense of alienation can be seen to extend to the furniture: "I sit me in my corner chair / That seems to feel itself from home".

Eliza Cook, a champion of workers' and women's rights, produced a journal in which, in 1851, when Clare was already ten years into his second and final long stint in an asylum, she produces a sketch of the poet. She conjectures that, far from doing him any favours, the literary fame he'd briefly enjoyed had only helped destabilise him:

> perhaps he finds he has mounted into a sphere where he has no natural supporters, where he is petted, patronized, borne with, perhaps spoiled, and where, severed from the class to which he naturally belonged, he floats adrift upon the surface of society, without a definite place or function – ill at ease, miserable, and sometimes *frantic with disappointment.*

"My friends forsake me like a memory lost": The simile, "me like a memory", unfolds to philosophical proportions. Do I exist only in as much as I appear in the memory of friends? Without them to remember who I am, how can I know? And the situation in the poem only gets worse: that memory where I have existed is *lost*. Although the inversion of the adjective "lost" is convenient in terms of rhyme, Clare is too deft a poet for it not to earn its place at the line end: "I am like a memory" would be one thing; "like a memory lost" is a whole other level of displacement, whose effects can be seen in reverse some eight lines later: "Even the dearest that I love the best / Are strange – nay, rather, stranger than the rest" (the half-rhyme, "lost" / "best", "rest", picks up the connection). So much depended on recognition that the loss of it renders those who were formerly "dearest", by a process of logical equivalence, the most strange.

The poem was beginning to seep into my being like prophecy. The weeks turned into months, and the months were beginning to tell. There's guilt – even as I toil up the back of the steep hill beyond my lane to take my daily exercise – that I am relatively unscathed; I am not on the breadline, retain my part-time job. But I am not immune. If, in this neck of the woods, the virus has yet to take a toll, I find I am acquiring it by proxy: the constant white noise that emanates from my computer screen, an unspecific feeling of persecution and dread. One day I come downstairs and the strawberries I'd left out on the side have been bound overnight in a fuzz of silver-white mould. Three months in and I fall out with a friend who was no friend, and, worse still, with a sister. We are all at the end of our tethers. This doesn't happen, it can't happen, it is too catastrophic. But there we are. The walls begin to cave in.

Clare had at least one sympathetic and instrumental friend in the asylum. William Knight became Head Steward in 1845. He took a keen interest in Clare's poetry, copying out over 800 pencilled drafts into neat copperplate, preserved to this day in two bound volumes in Northampton Central Library. Knight was key among a small band of well-meaning men that included Joseph Stenson, a partner in an iron-scrap works, and Thomas Inskip, a noted watchmaker and poetry lover. Between them, they encouraged and commented on Clare's writing.

Knight was the trusted amanuensis, and was keenly aware of the trust that was placed in him. He promised to copy out poems for Stenson on the understanding that the poems wouldn't be passed on, "for I fear I should not get any more by my transgressing of what ought to be kept sacred". In December 1846, he writes to Stenson telling him that he's sent Inskip, "that piece of Clare's 'I am'", which assumes that Stenson had already seen the poem. Inskip had been arranging to have odd poems of Clare's published in the *Bedford Times*.

The latest and most authoritative biography of Clare was published in 2003 by Jonathan Bate. Here, Bate attributes to the *Bedford Times* the same version of the poem that he also reproduces in his accompanying and newly edited edition of Clare's *Selected Poems*. Though a footnote in the biography mentions that there are "minor variants" to the text, I am surprised to see that the "frenzied stifled" line is present, and not entirely convinced. Or at least, I ask, if this is the earliest published version, where and when did that substitute line first creep in?

I can discover no documentary evidence online and seem to have hit a wall. But a friend more schooled in research than I am suggests I email the various libraries who hold the originals. I have been itching to see Knight's manuscript for myself, but, with travel restrictions, had given up any hope of doing so, imagining the library, in any case, would be shut. But I send off two speculative emails: one, requesting a copy of the relevant page of the local paper, and the other to the archivist at Northampton.

. . .

Meanwhile, William Knight has found another job, this time in Birmingham, and in 1849, he leaves Northampton. It is a desperate blow to Clare, who writes pitifully in 1850, "I am still wanting like Sternes Prisoners Starling to 'get out' but can't find the Way..."

That image of the starling from Sterne's *A Sentimental Journey* (1768) has by the nineteenth century become a cliché distinct from its literary origins (Maria Bertram conjures it in *Mansfield Park* (1814) to justify her flightiness around Henry Crawford). In the novel, Yorick, Sterne's happy-go-lucky protagonist, jokes about spending time "at the French King's expense" in the Bastille. The Bastille, he argues, can be no real hardship for "the terror is in the word. [...] the Bastile is but another word for a tower; – and a tower is but another word for a house you can't get out of." But he's interrupted in his musings by a sound from the hotel courtyard, where he is staying. At first he thinks it must be a child, but when he investigates further he finds a starling "hung in a little cage": "I cannot get out!" it repeats plaintively. Yorick attempts to free the bird, but to no avail, and is traumatised by the bird's distress. The episode punctures his frivolous, intellectual ideation, alerting him to the true *feeling* of what it must be like to be deprived of liberty. As a kind of penance, he devotes the whole of the following chapter to imagining the miseries of a human captive, wasting away in his prison cell.

Most readers might naturally ally themselves to Yorick, the teller of the tale, but Clare's identification is immediately with the captive. At least twice from Northampton he writes to his wife comparing the asylum to "the Bastile", where "I am in Prison", a place "where harmless people are trapped and tortured till they die". For Yorick the plight of the starling is a metaphorical prompt for the lot of a prisoner, but for Clare the two images are confounded and made literal: he envisions the reality of the captive's cell where prisoner and starling are thrown in together. By grammatical conflation ("Sternes Prisoners starling") the starling is restored to pole position, "harmless", "trapped", an allegiance that will be no surprise to anyone who has read Clare on the Badger, the Clock-a-Clay, the Snipe.

. . .

It isn't two days since I emailed the libraries and I'm amazed to find a reply from one waiting in my inbox: the team is currently working remotely, it says, *but it should be possible to direct a member of staff to the storage safe and to take a digital photo of the manuscript...*

The email fills me with delight. Something I have sent out blindly has found a mark, and, what's more, elicited a human response. I imagine the librarian at her desk, a respectable level of darkness, where, like mushrooms, books thrive. The smell is of spores and animal skins. I ring up to give my credit card details, and, businesslike though she is, am blessed by this unexpected interaction to the point of tears. In a couple of hours the jpeg arrives. Something holds me back from opening it, as if I've pushed my way through trouser-legs and coattails to the front of the room, where, suddenly, a space opens up and there's no one between myself and it, whatever it turns out to be.

Even though the encounter is virtual, there is a thrill at witnessing the curve of the page, the brown ink of the cursive italic, the pencilled emendations. Now I understand how irresistible it has been for editors to wade in. Is the pencil Clare's, or someone else's? Is it "oblivion host", "oblivious host" or "oblivion's host"? The most important line for me is there, but, again, not categorically so, crucial parts pencilled over or rubbed out: "Like shadows in love[] frenz[ied] stifled throes".

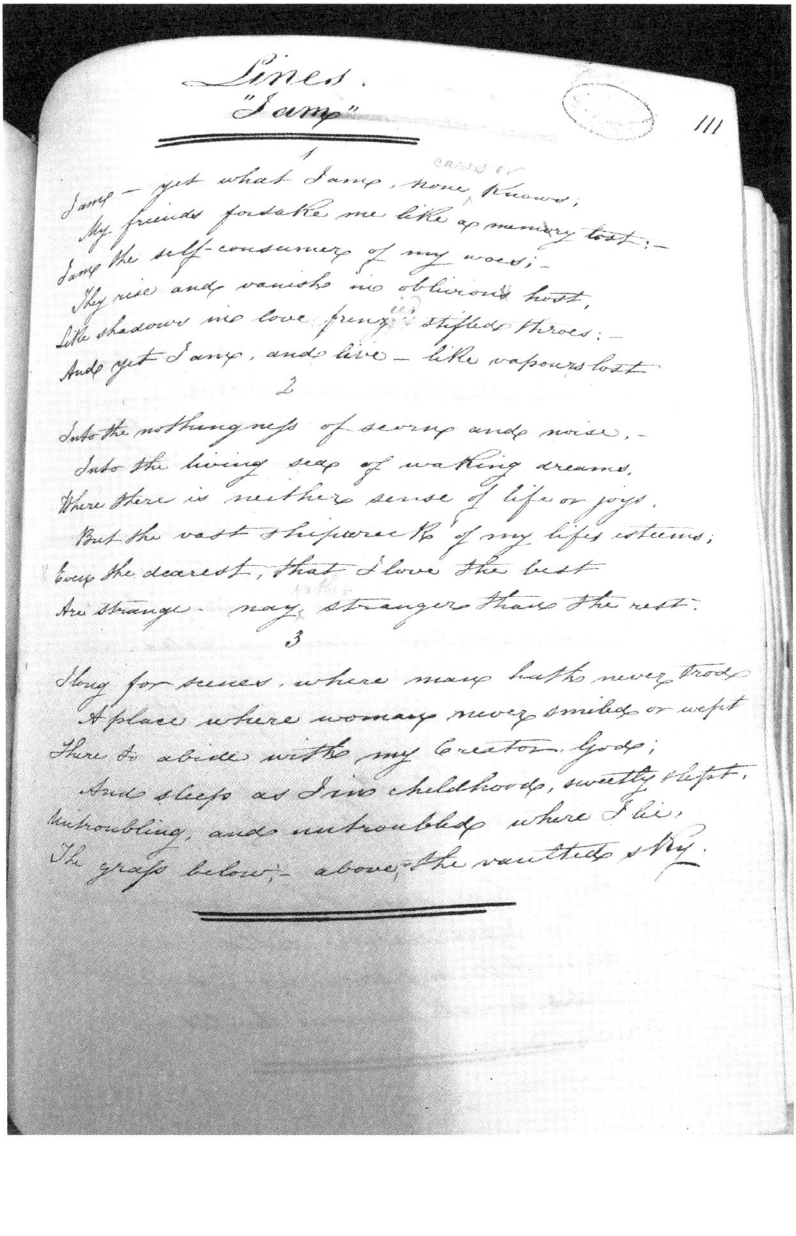

Lines.
"I am"

111

1

I am — yet what I am, none cares or knows;
My friends forsake me like a memory lost:—
I am the self-consumer of my woes;—
They rise and vanish in oblivions host,
Like shadows in love frenzies stifled throes:—
And yet I am, and live — like vapours tost

2

Into the nothingness of scorn and noise,—
Into the living sea of waking dreams,
Where there is neither sense of life or joys,
But the vast shipwreck of my lifes esteems;
Even the dearest, that I love the best
Are strange — nay, rather stranger than the rest.

3

I long for scenes, where man hath never trod
A place where woman never smiled or wept
There to abide with my Creator, God;
And sleep as I in childhood, sweetly slept,
Untroubling, and untroubled where I lie,
The grass below;— above, the vaulted sky.

John Clare's 'I am' copied out by William Knight. From the John Clare Collection, Northampton Central Library. Image by permission of Northamptonshire Libraries.

The second email arrives. This time, there's a copy, white against black, of the newspaper column of the *Bedford Times*, 1 January 1848. Here is Thomas Inskip's letter of recommendation, describing the poem as "a beam of light, beautiful in its loneliness, a mild ray gleaming through the shattered casement of a noble ruin!" But in the poem that follows the vital line has been replaced with "Like shades in Love and Death's oblivion tost". This is not, as Bate describes it, a minor textual variation, it is everything – this is where the poem has been de-sexed.

I can imagine now that between them, Inskip and Knight (perhaps, even, with Clare's assent) agree to opt for the more 'noble', printable line. And once established in print, this is the version that Dr Wing uses to mark Clare's dying, quoting it in full in his 1864 Annual Report of the Asylum, a version that is preserved more or less into the twentieth century through various editors, often poets – Norman Gale, Arthur Symons and Edmund Blunden – through the two-volume edition produced by J.W. Tibble in the 1930s, and ending up in the mid-'80s on a poster in the London Underground. It's a more polished version than the Frederick Martin and *Spectator* draft, but, like theirs, it is not the original.

Not until the end of August do I find myself sitting in a library, a paper mask strapped on for the duration. Unable to source the book online, I've ordered up Geoffrey Grigson's *Poems of John Clare's Madness* (1949). Grigson went back to look at the manuscripts for himself, and, as well as supplying new poems, says that he discovered "many differences of text" in those that had already been published. I am hopeful: page 132, 'I am'. I dive straight for the line, and there it is: "Like shadows in love's frenzied, stifled throes"! Over a hundred years since it was first conceived, a hundred years since someone took the trouble to go back and listen properly. Here is the moment the line enters the printed language. The circuit lights up, my glasses steam.

It is because the manuscripts are so scrappy, irregular in spelling and grammar, that they've offered a field day to editors, particularly those who want to stake a claim. In 1965, an academic, Eric Robinson, somehow managed to get his hands on the copyright in the published and unpublished works for a pound. He spent years working on editions of the poems, which would bring them back as close as they could be to the original unedited manuscripts. It was a Herculean labour, yet for his services he reserved an assumed right as copyright holder, a stranglehold on the reproduction of the poems that has only recently been loosened, and may explain why the doctored version of 'I am' of earlier editions persists even now.

Punctuation in the asylum poems is even less authoritative, relying on the vagaries of Knight's executive hand. It's possible at least to see how closely Jonathan Bate's latest version (a version used by Paul Farley in his 2007 *Selected*) corresponds to Knight's. The only distinctive variant is Bate's reading of the errant line, where (although he's not the first to do so) he converts "love" from a noun to a compound adjective, "love-frenzied".

The manuscript is rubbed in the critical places. But there is precedence in Knight for leaving out the possessive apostrophe: it isn't there, for instance, in line 9, in "lifes esteems". And the personification of love which the apostrophe confers ("Love's", as in Grigson) does not seem so far-fetched when, in the 1848 version, "Love" and "Death" are both embodied. That replacement line, "Like shades in love['s]", might be seen as a simple reworking of "Like shadows in love's". In terms of rhythm, too, that hyphen in "love-frenzied" defuses the full weight of the beat that otherwise hits the end of the line with such contrapuntal vigour: "*frenzied*, *stifled throes*". Such are the kinds of editorial quibble that have bedevilled Clare since he was first published.

Slipperiness was a feature of Clare's life as well as his work. Dr Nesbitt, one of the asylum doctors, observed:

> he may be said to have lost his own personal identity as with all the gravity of truth he would maintain that he had written the works of Byron, and Sir Walter Scott, that he was Nelson and Wellington, that he had fought and won the battle of Waterloo.

In a fragment called 'Self-Identity', written in about 1841, Clare reassures himself on the subject of changeablity: "I shall never be in three places at once," he says, "or ever change to a woman and that ought to be some comfort amid this moral or immoral 'changing' in life...". Mental aberration and genius: the element of madness is hard to gauge. But imagine if Clare had had access to Walt Whitman, only a generation younger, who in 1855 had published in *Leaves of Grass*, his 'Song of Myself': "I am large, I contain multitudes."

It was William Knight who recognised better than any of the doctors that the integrity of Clare's identity was bound up in his writing. Clare's mind, he observed, "must be employed in writing poetry or Clare will be Clare no longer."

I don't know what I've achieved, if anything, in beavering away at the poem, squirrelling out the variant and deviant versions, hampered by the extent to which I could find texts online. But I do know that in the memorialising of it and the thinking about it, I have not been lonely. I am not John Clare, not struggling to keep my family clothed and fed, hobbled by mental illness, so much so that my wife, for the second time, has me consigned to the asylum, where I will live, chewing tobacco, for the last twenty-three years of my life. I am not, and yet it's possible to feel that I am. I learn and recite each line as if it is a combination that one by one will give me a clearer understanding of myself.

There's a field I love to walk in. It lies at exactly the same angle as a field I played in as a child. I remember skipping down as if someone else was there beside me, watching how well I negotiated the tussocks and dips, looking forward to a time when I was grown up and that person would materialise and be with me.

It didn't turn out that way. And yet, walking the field again, slantwise, I can feel a presence, someone who knows the names of every single flower, thistle, clover. And I'm reminded by the angle of the field, which allows me to believe in a world that is round and not flat, of the carefree hopefulness between field and sky, as close as possible to the feeling of being held by gravity from falling off.

Essay

AUDIBILITY IN THE ARCHIVE

Langston Hughes and Sylvia Plath's Poetry for Radio

Nerys Williams

Back in the mid-'90s, my line manager, an archivist at the Film and Sound Library at BBC Wales, told me an anecdote. Some years before, the entire archive had to be reorganised, material was to be culled, space on the Cardiff campus had become a premium. These were the days of quarter-inch audiotape and editing by razor blade. Recorded sound was still a physical object, preserved in cardboard boxes, catalogued by year, week and programme number. The refurbishment contract necessitated a quick turnaround, which meant that radio producers were under pressure to authorise what materials they wanted kept. A skip had been brought to the back of the archive, and was filling fast. Alarmed by the mini mountain of white boxes that were massing, one evening my boss took a stepladder and climbed into the skip to sift through the reels. Programmes in both Welsh and English were rescued. Some were archived as compilation tapes under the acronym WAL (Wales Audio Library). From one archive another devolved one emerged.

Archives represent a curating of values, be they aesthetic, cultural or historical. In *Archive Fever: A Freudian Impression* (1996, translated by Eric Prenowitz) Jacques Derrida emphasises that 'archive' is etymologically linked to ideas of power and authority. He reflects that the word's Greek source *arkheion* originally meant "a house, a domicile, an address, the residence of the superior magistrates, the archons, those who commanded. The citizens who thus held and signified political power were considered to possess the right to make or to represent the law." Archives offer an important cultural narrative; they are protected spaces which are simultaneously public and private. While archives may purport to tell us an official or sanctioned history, they are also invariably defined by their absences: items that are missing, destroyed, lost and and/or in many cases devalued and thrown away.

To any researcher, archives are seductive spaces. They offer the possibility of a new scrap of knowledge, the challenge of deciphering marginalia, and in the case of some early BBC memos, an encounter with unvarnished opinion. Over the past three years I have been spending some time in BBC archives again, hunting down the history of collaborations between poets and producers at the BBC's Third Programme (1946–67). I have sifted through programme paperwork, memos, letters and scripts as well as listening to programmes in small booths. It has frequently been a visceral process: in Bloomington, Indiana handling Christmas cards, BBC listeners' reports, drawings and programme brochures; memos, letters and drafts of programme ideas in Caversham. Susan Howe in *Spontaneous Particulars: The Telepathy of Archives* (2014) reminds us that there is an important tactile dimension to working with archival material, one that cannot be replicated digitally. Howe states that "electronic technologies are radically transforming the way we read, write and remember" and poses that "the nature of archival research itself is in flux". She affirms that "we need to see and touch objects and documents; now we often merely view the same material on a computer screen". Howe captures this moment of seeing as an instant of transformative energy. The item that was once shut carefully away "outside an economy of use, inaccessible to touch" becomes "re-animated, re-collected (recollected) through an encounter with the mind of a curious reader, a researcher, an antiquarian, a bibliomaniac, a sub sub-librarian, a poet."

My research on poets and BBC radio producers at the Third Programme has brought me to focus on D.G. Bridson's editorial partnership with Langston Hughes in 1963–4 and Douglas Cleverdon's commissioning of work by Sylvia Plath in 1962. Bridson was a poet and a visionary producer of the radio feature programme. He started as a freelance writer, then joined BBC radio as a Feature Programmes Assistant (North Region) in 1935. His early programmes represented working-class lives through documentary forms such as in his three radio features – *Coal, Cotton People* and *Wool*, all broadcast in 1938. Crucially, Bridson saw himself as a disseminator of new poetry and aligned himself to a particular challenge of modernist poetic experimentation, which spanned the high modernism of T.S. Eliot and Ezra Pound to the poetics of the Harlem Renaissance in Langston Hughes's poetry. Cleverdon is best known for his work as the producer of *Under Milk Wood* in 1954, joining BBC radio in 1939 following a career in book publishing. Recruited by Laurence Gilliam as a feature producer for the newly formed BBC Third Programme, Cleverdon encouraged new poets to produce new works specially written for radio. His unpublished manuscript *The Art of Radio* examines the role of the radio producer as offering mentorship and practical guidance to poets. Cleverdon's collaborations with Dylan Thomas, David Gascoyne and Plath were all commissioned works from the BBC's radio features department. He asserted that radio was conducive to poetic exploration: "Radio is *par excellence* the medium for the poet – not merely in its simplest form of enabling him to read his own poems aloud to his listeners. There is in radio no limit to the evocative power of words; it is the medium of the ear alone."

Writing for Radio: Poets in Early Broadcasting

In 1936 Rudolf Arheim proposed that "Poets should emphatically be brought into the wireless studio, for it is much more conceivable that they should be able to adapt a verbal work of art to the limits of space, sound and music." Collaboration between poets and radio producers has an established history at the BBC. From the late 1930s, the BBC offered staff contracts to several poets as writers, broadcasters, and producers, including Louis MacNeice, Rayner Heppenstall and Geoffrey Grigson. For many cultural commentators of the 1930s and '40s, radio provided poets not only with the possibility of a responsive new audience but also of re-examining poetry's relationship with a culture of communal speech. In his 1938 open letter, Herbert Read stated: "There must be many experiments, not only with the compositions of poems but in the speaking of poems [...]. We must get rid of the idea that poetry can be read, or announced, or even recited." Read stressed not only the importance of reshaping the performative aspect of poetry but also the necessity for presenting poetry as a socially relevant art form on the air: "Poetry must be composed by the voice [...]. It must be treated as a new art – an art to be discovered by vast circles of dumb listeners. This would be a means of saving poets from a solipsistic 'underground life'."

Famously George Orwell's 1945 pamphlet *Poetry and the Microphone* proposed that "by being set down at a microphone, especially if this happens at all regularly, the poet is brought into a new relationship with his work". Poetry's engagement with radio releases it from print, as well as offering a possible freedom from "that grisly thing – a poetry reading". However, for Orwell, poetry on the air still "sounds like the Muses in striped trousers", as he points out that "one ought not to confuse the capabilities of an instrument with the use it is actually put to".

The Third established an ambitious role in cultural programming in broadcasting history. In the words of the BBC Director General William Haley, its content was to "be directed to an audience that is not of one class, but that is perceptive and intelligent". Three years prior, in 1943, the BBC had set up the Literary Output Committee. The Committee since its inception had attempted to address how poetry should be better adapted to the radio. Regarding future poetry input, the Committee proposed that radio should serve "as a platform" for new verse not only from Great Britain "but from the Dominions and the Empire and a platform for which poets would willingly write poetry designed for broadcast and to be spoken aloud". The Third Programme offered an experimental premise which promoted new writing for radio.

Both Bridson and Cleverdon were attuned to radio's potential as a disseminator of cultural commentary and narrative of potential political change to a mass audience, as well as its possibility to create new radiogenic forms which pushed the limits and expectations of a more 'traditional' poetry reading audience. Often these new productions offered innovative sonic performances, provocative representations of subjectivity and taboo subject material. The 'radio feature' as an emergent (and fluid) genre enabled forms of experimentation that combined poetry, speech, music, sound effects and actuality. As producers, Bridson and Cleverdon enabled what Séan Street refers to as a "*poetics*" of radio making. Street comments on producers and poets' creation of the "radio poem" as a work whose "intention [...] is based on sound, the radio poem has been created first and foremost to be *listened* to". This acute awareness of how the texts were written, produced, listened to and received is what I reflect upon on reading and listening to Langston Hughes and Sylvia Plath's radio broadcasts.

Langston Hughes: Jericho-Jim Crow *(1964)*

Recent research on the evolution of BBC radio and its relationship to empire has begun to articulate the often invisible history of race at the institution. Critical studies have brought to attention the history of Caribbean writers at the BBC. These texts place a focus on the politics of race at the institution, especially in the case of Una Marston who was both a poet and a BBC producer. They also remind a researcher of the importance of mining the BBC's archive to disseminate overlooked histories or voices integral to understanding the cultural and political conditions of the institution.

Langston Hughes was approached by Bridson as co-editor of the ambitious nineteen-part radio series *The Negro in America*, broadcast in autumn 1964. The premise of their collaboration might initially seem unusual, given Bridson's strong affiliations to a strand of Anglo-American Modernism, made evident by his close friendships and BBC productions with Wyndham Lewis and Ezra Pound. Hughes and Bridson nurtured a strong friendship, having been introduced to one another by Alan Lomax. However, the BBC itself had not always welcomed Hughes's poetry. Indeed one memo written on 24 November 1943 from the BBC Copyright department reveals that Hughes's famous poem 'The Negro Speaks of Rivers' was taken out of a broadcast since they decided that the poem was not worth the broadcast fee asked.

Bridson and Hughes had collaborated closely with one another before. In 1944 Bridson commissioned and produced Hughes's ballad opera *The Man Who Went to War*, which included an introduction voiced by Paul Robeson. Set in London during the Blitz but performed exclusively by African American voices, the production offered a rethinking of the war propaganda programming. Earlier BBC series such as *The Stones Cry Out* (1941) had performed an important role in affirming wartime nationalistic pride. *The Stones Cry Out* looked at the damage inflicted on individual buildings in the UK by aerial bombing. Each episode ended with an assertion of plucky British courage: "The Stones Cry Out – But the People Stand Firm." By contrast, *The Man Who Went to War* superimposed the experience of African American life, culture and experience upon a blitzed

London. Bridson commented that "By turning London into Harlem, two things became possible; firstly we could give wartime London a look at itself through Negro eyes; and secondly, we could give it a chance to imagine the Negro's own struggle." Robeson's prelude offers empathy which is informed by an intergenerational experience of racism and expressed through the idiom of folk and gospel:

> Because we have felt the pathos and the anger of war in our own hearts, we are acting and singing our story for you in the way that is natural to us. We are giving you a picture of what you yourselves have lived through, Britain – only the words and songs are our own.

The Negro in America (1964) was a monumental series for the Third. In its programming we can see that Hughes, with Bridson, is attempting to place into context the struggle of civil rights and integration in the USA for a UK audience. The series offers a rich introduction to the history and legacy of African American cultural production in the US and the world. Hughes fronted several programmes in the series: a roundtable on African American writing and a curated anthology of African American poetry, and his own work and political activism was profiled in an extensive interview with Bridson. But possibly most innovative was his adaptation for broadcast of his gospel play *Jericho-Jim Crow*. The play originated with the Greenwich Mews Theatre and played the Sanctuary of The Village Presbyterian Church and Brotherhood Synagogue in New York. Bridson brokered a deal for the BBC; in exchange for the rights to broadcast *Jericho-Jim Crow*, the BBC paid towards the professional recording of the drama by Folkways recordings. *Jericho-Jim Crow* was Hughes's civil rights play and he dedicated the work to "young people of all racial and religious backgrounds who are meeting, canvassing, petitioning, marching, picketing, sitting in, singing and praying today to help make a better America for all, and especially for citizens of color". Profits from the original live performances were split between the Congress for Racial Equality, Student Non Violence Coordinating Committee and the NAACP.

In the essay 'Gospel Singers: New Asset to American Theatre 1963' Hughes describes the process of writing his successful gospel song play *Black Nativity* (1961). During this time Hughes was revisiting the experimental intersection of folk and gospel music that had informed the structure of *The Man Who Went to War*. Hughes visited gospel temples in

Harlem late at night and described the combination of song and drama:

> A mingling of ancient scripture and contemporary problems were projected with melodic intensity and rhythmic insistence. Every night I was drawn into the circle of oneness generated by the basic beat of the gospel tempo.

Creating a transhistorical stage is central to the dynamics of *Jericho-Jim Crow*. The gospel play delineates a passage from slavery to integration and the civil rights movement. Jim Crow is presented as a white Trickster figure shifting across time and identities; he is slave owner and trader, Klansman and jailor. Gospel singing performs the role of a classic Greek chorus, enabling singers to comment collectively on action in the play. Hughes was mesmerised by the sense of a shared space generated by gospel singing; his essays stress the intersubjective force that singers generate with their audience. For Hughes gospel singers are "masters of drama, they delight at improvising on the mood of their audiences as well as on the music itself".

Jericho-Jim Crow's incorporation of traditional gospel songs creates a historical narrative across centuries tracing a movement from civil war folk song 'John Brown's Body', post-civil war freedom song 'Oh Freedom', Underground Railroad song 'Follow the Drinking Gourd' to 'Slavery Chain', an African American spiritual said to have been composed shortly after Lincoln's Emancipation Proclamation of 1 January 1863. Near the end, the play combines narratives of protest and civil disobedience with an emphatic refrain of "We shall overcome".

Hughes's vast historical soundscape of African American history is also replicated in the multiple identities represented in the gospel drama. One of his characters, "Young Girl", is a transhistorical freedom fighter generated from revolutionary African American women who campaigned for freedom, race equality and women's suffrage:

> GIRL My name is Harriet Tubman Sojourner Truth Mary Church Terrell Ida Wells Barnett Mary McLeod Bethune Autherine Lucy Rosa Parks Daisy Bates Dianne Nash Charlayne Hunter Juanita Malone Anniebelle Smith – that's me, and a lot more names too – taken from you. But for short you call me Anniebelle. And folks I'm on my way.

The BBC's listeners' reports for *Jericho-Jim Crow* were enthusiastic; listeners commented on how moved they were by the narrative, they also praised its compelling political message. The broadcasting of *Jericho-Jim Crow* enabled Hughes to give voice to a brutal racial history while also offering an intimate and direct appeal to his audience through gospel performance.

Sylvia Plath, Three Women *(1962)*

In 1962 Plath's *Three Women* was commissioned by Cleverdon and the features department, not by the radio drama department. This distinction is an important one. The features department was recognised as having a strong history of advocating writing for radio which experimented with the medium itself, as opposed to relying on adaptations from literary texts. For Cleverdon, feature programmes had key radiogenic characteristics: "The feature is the only form of radio programme which does not derive from some external source such as the theatre, the concert hall, the pulpit, the lecture-room, or the music-hall." As the late historian of the BBC Asa Briggs notes, there was an "intimate connection between feature writing and poetry", with the development of this genre being furthered by the close relationship established between poets and producers with an interest in experimenting with its broadcast form.

Plath's *Three Women* strategically uses the 'intimacy' of radio listening as an opportunity to perform a powerful social and public comment on the experiences of childbirth, abortion and disability to a listening public. The poet balances a relationship between a 'play of ideas' and establishing a lyric intensity with her audience; this radio drama is often evaluated as offering a stylistic bridge between *The Colossus* and *Ariel*. *Three Women* was billed in the *Radio Times* as the "Soliloquies of three women in a maternity ward". Plath's three female speakers remain consciously unnamed. The first woman's marital status and occupation is unspecified; she gives birth to a son. The second speaker, often referred to by critics as a married secretary, enters the ward miscarrying her child. The third, a student, is carrying a child but chooses to have her daughter adopted. In a letter to her mother Plath specifies that the three monologues began as a working through of Ingmar Bergman's film *Brink of Life* (1958). Bergman's film focuses on three female patients' experiences on a maternity ward: Cecilia who is struggling to overcome a miscarriage, Hjordis who has attempted to abort her unborn child, and Stina who enthusiastically awaits the birth of her baby only to lose her child in a traumatic birthing scene.

Plath's radio play is tailored towards three different voices; in the production this was to be emphasised through the choice of readers. However, two of the three readers engaged for the production were, at the last moment, unable to take part. Cleverdon comments that as a consequence "the voices were not as differentiated as they should have been", an issue which is echoed in the feedback from BBC listeners' reports. Plath's *Three Women* draws inspiration from Bergman's intimate consideration of the traumas of medical experience for women; his filmic technique of often painful close-ups is mirrored in Plath's choice of the soliloquy as framing device for her own portraits. However, one distinguishing feature between them is that there is that no interaction between the women on Plath's ward. The discovery and sharing of personal narratives forms a key factor of the women's healing in Bergman's film. Plath's use of the soliloquy form as a framework enables us to experience moments of intense subjectivity and the shifts in lyric time associated with physical and mental trauma. In this way, *Three Women* enables taboo material to find enunciation in a public realm.

In a late interview Plath insisted that "I feel that this development of recording poems, of speaking poems at readings, of having records of poets" offer a return to "the old role of the poet, which was to speak to a group of people". Plath's work displays an acute understanding of the technical requirements of radio writing required by her producer. Plath was already familiar with Cleverdon's work; in 1962 he produced Ted Hughes's first radio drama, *The Wound*. Cleverdon emphasises that after his collaboration with Hughes it was "natural" that "the idea should emerge of a radio piece by Sylvia Plath also". A BBC memo on 16 May 1962 confirms that Cleverdon is happy with the commission and a contract for a script of fifty-four seven-line stanzas is requested by the producer. This sense of a text being written *exclusively* for radio, is crucial to understanding Plath's *Three Women*, with its dependence on the soliloquy as a compelling form for engaging the listener. The work examines difficult subjects: childbirth, miscarriage and adoption.

There is an intersubjective dynamic that is created between the speaking voice and listener. For Cleverdon the microphone offers "an extraordinary sympathetic means of expression to the dramatist who has something to say or something to discuss which he convinces could be made interesting to an audience of millions." The time constraints of a radio play create an intensity of listening and Plath recontextualises the key words for different nuance and effect in the three soliloquies. For the first voice, the motif of whiteness relates to the impending birth, it offers a spot of reflective time where time stands still: "The sheets, the faces are white and stopped, like clocks." By comparison, for the second voice the whiteness of the hospital sheets evokes the erasure of potential life itself "like the faces of my children". For the third voice whiteness is associated with actions that appear beyond her control, attributed to the "white, cold wing" of conception. Whiteness is also associated with the operating theatre as a white horror chamber filled with surgical instruments and sounds of pain. One could add that the colour red serves to mark moments of crucial narrative development in the broadcast. Red for the first voice associated with the postnatal body and placenta, "a red lotus opens in its bowl of blood". For the second it is the evidence of a miscarriage which starts as a seep of blood and at the close, red offers a return to a performative identity, the lipstick on "the old mouth". Red for the third voice symbolises the impossibility of being a mother to the "red terrible girl" with a head carved in "red, hard wood".

Three Women offers a challenge to more conventional forms of radio drama. Plath refuses to provide a direct linear narrative leading to a moment of epiphanic understanding. Undoubtedly, there are moments of climax in the text, which coincide with the first voice's pain at birth, the second voice's loss and the third's preparation for adoption. But there are other crosscurrents in the text which resist a definitive representation of maternal experience; the script defies a plot-based narrative that is propelled by cause and effect.

Feedback from the BBC's listeners' reports offers an insight into the tensions created by *Three Women*. Those critical of the broadcast thought that while the radio programme's excursion into morbid psychological states was perceptive, the overwhelming result was too intimate for a listening public. Acknowledging the intersubjective exchange created by *Three Women* is key to understanding the poetics of listening that Plath and Cleverdon produced. A perception of intimacy is crucial to the delivery of the soliloquy, and is also a key characteristic of radio drama's "theater of mind". A sense of articulation and listening as an intimate and private act is encapsulated by the first voice's statement "I talk to myself, myself only". We are reminded that *Three Women* was broadcast to a mass audience of public listeners. At this time it is estimated that the average audience for the Third Programme was a million and a half listeners.

As George Orwell notes in *Poetry and the Microphone*, there is a paradox inherent to radio broadcasting: "Millions may be listening, but each is listening alone." In producing a radiogenic text, Plath is required to enunciate a complex balancing act between private and public life. In *Jericho-Jim Crow* Hughes uses gospel drama as a way of suturing the burden of history, while enabling the agency of the individual voice. For Hughes and Plath their collaborations with the BBC created works which present sound as what Jonathan Sterne calls "an artifact of the messy and political human sphere".

WHITE IS NOT A RACIAL SLUR

Claudia Rankine, Just Us: An American Conversation, *Allen Lane, £25,* *ISBN 9780241467107*

Kayo Chingonyi on listening, asking, and seeing

. . .

> *I think if there is one thing my work does, one thing it's invested in, it's seeing. What does it mean to see this thing happen?*
>
> Claudia Rankine interviewed by Kayo Chingonyi in *The White Review*

One of the most contentious aspects in the study of race, and its operations, is the re-examination of the privileged status of whiteness. While many critical race theorists believe it is crucial to demote whiteness from the position of centrality, to destabilise its status as the normative subject position, there is also the feeling that focusing too closely on whiteness gives further time and space to a subjectivity which has already a great deal of capital in terms of its predominance as a stand-in for being in the world. How often, for example, do we (and who, indeed, are "we"?) assume, when we read a descriptive passage in which a character's race is elided, that this means the character is white?

I want here, perhaps mistakenly, to take a departure into the *Harry Potter* series. In my work as a teacher of creative writing, it has been staggering to observe first-hand the influence of these books on a new generation of writers, many of whom were born in the ten years between the publication of the first book in the series and the last. Why do I mention these books? Like it or not they have transcended the cul-de-sac of literary culture and influenced the wider fabric. I wonder, then, if this influence goes beyond the lexical dimension, which sees "muggle" as a genuine catchall for the uninitiated, to include, also, the manner in which a character's race is depicted. Isn't it troubling that even in this magical fictive world, where it is possible to disappear from one place and reappear somewhere else, the author still finds it necessary to make clear that certain characters are not white even as she fails to render the whiteness of dominant characters visible? Of what is this invisibility emblematic?

These are the kinds of questions Claudia Rankine proffers in *Just Us*, a book written in the documentary poetic style for which Rankine is justifiably celebrated. And here we have our first point of discussion. To what extent is *Just Us* a poetry book? While there are the cross-modal traces we find in *Don't Let Me Be Lonely* (2004) and *Citizen* (2014), of a relation between poetry and other art forms, there is the feeling in this latest volume that the matter of whether or not this is a book of poetry is even less important than the transformative nature of the work in which the book is engaged. While there are texts we can recognise as poems here, the lion's share of paginated extent is given over to a prose form that is conspicuously light on the kinds of linguistic effects we might think of as *uniquely poetic*. And yet, once again, Rankine is engaged, in *Just Us* as in *Citizen*, in the mining of experience to find the punctum; in the employment of poetic narrative economy, that mode of writing which encourages the reader to co-create a text's meaning. So, if this is not exactly a book of poems, does it comport itself sufficiently to be considered a book of poetry? A good question on which perhaps only the process of reading can shed meaningful light:

> After hanging up the phone, I walked to my front door and opened it. The lawn was covered by fallen leaves. For all its apparent beauty the dead leaves were rotting. Staring into the leaves, I remembered that weeks before a white woman said to me, "I've been doing antiracist work since the eighties. I'm here to tell you it makes no difference." In the moment I laughed with my full face. My laughter was so embodied she started to laugh as well.

There is much to unpack here but I am struck immediately by the plain style. The manner in which a poem's tendency to heighten experience is being subverted in order to render the banality of the moment explicit. This is not, I think, coincidental. How better to show the unthinking operations of a societal structure than by holding it up for scrutiny and letting the reader draw their own conclusions rather than the jab-in-the-ribs-geddit effect that more conspicuous stylistic choices would invoke. There is a complication here, though, because of course presenting this passage in the context of poetic work is an audacious, and therefore conspicuous, thing to do. But how else to do justice to the matter in hand? Our recently departed Kamau Brathwaite told us "the hurricane does not roar in pentameter" and in so doing challenged us to find the particular occasion of each poetic utterance. It is this that Rankine is doing in the anecdotal, episodic form she adopts in *Just Us*. Certainly, there will be a sense of disappointment for the reader who seeks for a poet to render experience in mellifluous tones, but for the reader who seeks for the poet to "add to the stock of available reality" (to conjure R.P. Blackmur for a moment) this capacious volume offers manifold gifts.

There was, for this reader at least, the sense that *Just Us* is intended as a conversation starter. It is necessarily unfinished in the sense that it offers no final conclusions except to reaffirm the importance of stepping outside the comfort of orthodoxy and like-mindedness to stand in the spaces where racial difference is in sharpest relief and to weather the discomfort of so doing in order to ask questions. It is striking that much of the text concerns itself with giving voice to white people, to finding out about them:

> I reminded myself that I was there only to listen. Just listen.
>
> Maybe our social work becomes our attempt to be in relation. Conversations should be redefined as such.
>
> What I know is that an inchoate desire for a future other than the one that seems to be forming our days brings me to a seat around any table to lean forward, to hear, to respond, to await response from any other.

As with previous volumes, the subtitle of the book hints at its formal qualities and so in *Just Us* we are presented with the poetics of listening, of exchange. There is less of the sense of apportioning blame or seeking accountability but rather a renewed emphasis on the importance of curiosity and openness in the uncomfortable process of doing anti-racist work. The central project of the book, then, is to extend across racial divides the hand of kinship in the hope of highlighting a shared humanity. The book makes clear the cost of such a position to black people but also elucidates the importance of mutual compassion to processes of change. If *Citizen* sought to make clear that change was a necessity, *Just Us* looks at what that change might look like, how we might begin the process of bringing it about.

In *Just Us* Claudia Rankine aligns herself with those critical race theorists who believe that a robust interrogation of whiteness and its structures is crucial to anti-racist work. The overwhelming impression one gets from reading the book is that it is not enough merely to look at isolated instances of, say, privilege or racism, but rather that one must look at who has privilege and why. One must look at the direction in which capital flows and why. Through the book, Rankine posits that the existing structures are insufficient to the task of precipitating change and so we must enter a more uncomfortable process in which we never become complacent. Here, Rankine embarks on the audacious, perennial task of doing just that.

Kayo Chingonyi is the author of Kumukanda *(Chatto, 2017) and Poetry Editor at* The White Review.

SIDEBURNS

Alexander Pushkin, Selected Poetry, *translated by Antony Wood, Penguin, £10.99,* *ISBN 9780241207130*

Alistair Noon on the Russian poet's exclamations and exhortations

. . .

Age-wise not quite the Mozart of poetry, but a precocious writer and voracious reader, Alexander Pushkin (1799–1837) was producing more or less mature poetry at an age at which you wouldn't expect most poets to be mature as people, let alone as poets (fourteen). His saturation of the Russian cultural market lacks an exact Anglophone counterpart: Shakespeare's dramas go Hollywood, but how many Tennysonian tales have become animated films? Besides prose, he wrote lyric, narrative and dramatic poetry in both high-brow and folksy variants, and developed hybrid forms. Bar the prose, all these are represented in Antony Wood's major new selection and translation.

Pushkin's a one-stop shop for what's scattered elsewhere before, during and after his time: Horatian stateliness, Wordsworthian humility, Byronic disreputableness, Shelleyan politicisation, Keatsian aestheticism, Heinean balladity and Poe-ean goth-horror. Practically any communicative act seems transmutable to verse for him: a final warning for a gambling debt, or telling off friends pressing him to get a move on with his verse novel *Eugene Onegin* (not excerpted here: you can't have everything in a Selected). The metapoem or metapoetic aside holds no fear for Pushkin, anticipating by a century and a half Denise Levertov's caution that if we expect poets to write from experience, we shouldn't be dismissive when poets write about the experience of writing.

Exclamations on ephemerality and exhortations of consolation jostle epigrams on reactionaries and epistles to progressives (often in the Siberian exile which Pushkin, as a sympathiser with the abortive Decembrist revolt of 1825, was lucky to escape). There are rants at censors, reactions to mates' new books, excoriations of unsatisfactory plays, spats with one-time Polish poetry pal Adam Mickiewicz, and dry runs for the opening of Pushkin's most resonant narrative poem, 'The Bronze Horseman', included here. Unsolicited advice, toasts and admonitions to top up the glasses, virtual school reunions, sober reflections on diplomatic careers, lampoons of miserly priests and repressed monks, portraits, parodies, pastorals and Ozymandian parables join frequent declarations of admiration and confessions of infatuation.

The simplicity attributed to Pushkin can be reformulated as his capacity to synthesise emotions: I fancied you, it hurt, and I still fancy you, but don't let that bug you, I hope you find someone else. Or: loving you's a waste of time, pretend you love me, I'm easy to deceive and happy to deceive myself. Or as his capacity to evoke a time and place very precisely: waking up to a winter landscape by turns invigorating and desolate. Diction can be complex in Pushkin's riffs on classical models and metres (one cannot rhyme all the time) and political odes. The latter include the rumblings of a mainstream Russian ambivalence to the West, admiration mixed with disgruntlement at taking geopolitical hits for it (Genghis Khan, Napoleon, and eventually Hitler), echoed in Alexander Blok's 'Scythians' of 1918, as Russia bailed out of the First World War, and more indirectly in 1992, in Joseph Brodsky's unpublished but eyebrow-raising 'On the Independence of the Ukraine'.

In Pushkin's popular early lyrics, the first-person singular is recognisably very first person, often with notes to self or adjurements that such and such is not meant. As Pushkin loses followers and his relationship status gets more complicated, the tone turns from joy to despair. As if the answer is to dissolve the self in the writing, dramatic monologues arrive and translations, versions and imitations revive, drawing inter alia on contemporary English romantics, such as the now obscure Barry Cornwall, whose day job was Commissioner in Lunacy.

It's an oddity of translation that reputations bob up in bottles from source cultures, but the letter inside immediately raises its own questions: the genie's out, but is it a genius? The oddity is compounded where time dilation occurs: some translations put Pushkin into Byronese, for example, asking an allowance too far of readers already making allowances. One approach to verse translation sets relatively high store on reflecting the relative regularity of source form, though making its own necessary and productive compromises. Unsurprisingly, this is asking for inverted syntax, conflicts of natural and metrical stress, and pressure on idiomaticity (if the latter's what you're after), all of this in tension with the desirability of historicising the language in translation or not.

What's more surprising is that – with enough other skills in the mix – this doesn't matter that much. There are poems and passages in this volume which, given the parameters set and followed consistently though not inflexibly, this reviewer feels may not, in isolation, thoroughly convince unbelievers of Pushkin's rounded power and strategic directness. But there are many more where this is much more likely:

It is October, and the lingering leaves
Are disappearing from the naked branches;
The road is glazed, the cold of autumn breathes;
The millstream still sounds loudly as it passes,
But now the pond is hard; out in the fields
My neighbour urges on his canine forces,
The frenzied sport disturbs the winter crops,
And sleeping groves are roused by baying dogs.
('Autumn (A fragment)')

What often truly glues a verse translation together is non-choppiness, allied with adequate lexical density and metrical flexibility, and that's certainly the case here (it's clear from the introduction that the tactics derive from extensive reflection and experience). The edition includes highly knowledgeable introductory material and notes giving numerous insights into the poems' literary, publishing, social and political contexts. Where the notes detail formal divergences from the original, this is informative (and common practice) but risks strengthening some readers' socioculturally conditioned expectation that translations are ipso facto deficient (sometimes so locally, but much less so globally, given enough compensation): as the great translation theorist Ronald Reagan said, if you're explaining, you're losing.

"Because in my harsh age I sang of Liberty, / And asked, for the fallen, lenience" ('Exegi monumentum'): Pushkin's prospective self-elegy plagiarises Horace, but the meme is his and shared a century later by Bertolt Brecht:

> You, however, when the time comes
> When mankind is a helper to mankind
> Think on us
> With forbearance.
>
> ('To those born after', translated by Tom Kuhn)

Who are "the fallen"? Wood's translation usefully expands the original's sense of "sinners" to include soldiers (why not, it makes sense). Pushkin displays the tensions of progressivism and nationalism in the early nineteenth century, when the nation still meant the people versus the monarch. Who exactly is this Liberty for?

His purview is not narrow, but still selective. "Gypsies" (ie Roma and Sinti) are free by nature. Greeks deserve freedom from the Ottomans (which, coincidentally, is in Russia's geopolitical interest), while Poles in the Russian Empire should stop moaning, Adam. The dial also wobbles on antisemitism, with awareness of Jewish poverty combined with use of disparaging language. Pushkin doesn't escape his time's specific stereotypes of women, usually ladies, madams or nannies, though there's more depth to female figures in *Eugene Onegin*, as you'd expect given the novel (in both senses) form. Intelligence in a woman is neither excluded nor expected, discussions of politics are with male interlocutors, there's self-aggrandisement but little machismo. Even where refracted through exoticist droplets, as in 'The Fountain of Bakhchisaray', a tale of two harem inmates, there is a consistent implication of female autonomy in the sexual sphere, acknowledgement of violence against women ('The Bridegroom'), and sympathy with women left in the reproductive lurch.

'The Gypsies' is a tale of both ethnic and gender freedom, if also, again, a projection (the back story has a mother abandon her daughter). Here, Pushkin himself problematises the selectivity of liberty: "Not for freedom were you born, / You want it for yourself alone..." the Old Man tells Aleko, the Russian partner-murderer. It explores the interplay of freedom and justice, as 'The Bronze Horseman' counterpoints the individual and the State. The latter poem is indeed not Peter the Great's but Pushkin's own memorial, visible across later Russian literature. Anna Akhmatova wrote that Pushkin "triumphed over space and time". For Russians, there's no doubt regarding the time. With their fresh flowers on the monument, these translations expand the space.

And he had great sideburns.

Alistair Noon's translations of Osip Mandelstam, Concert at a Railway Station, *were published by Shearsman in 2018. He lives in Berlin.*

THINGS NOT FOUND IN BOOKS

Ariana Reines, A Sand Book, *Penguin, £12.99,* *ISBN 9780141992693*
Carolyn Forché, In the Lateness of the World, *Bloodaxe, £10.99,* *ISBN 9781852249649*

Dzifa Benson on soothsaying, visions and reportage

...

Reading Ariana Reines' *A Sand Book* is a delightfully disorienting experience. It's akin to being tipped into audacious, libidinous, quixotic, queer chaos that manages, somehow, to be measured too. In a previous book, *Mercury* (2011), Reines wrote, "writing beautifully made me feel like a fake". If Reines weren't such a charismatically intelligent writer, the poetry in this book could have easily collapsed under the weight of its own edifice. This poetry collection isn't just vast in sheer size, it is also vast in its ambition to contain multitudes dating back millennia, to knit time together into a contemporaneous past, present and future. Weighing in at a whopping 400 pages and 136 lyric poems – not counting the images that preface each of the 12 sections which include the veve, or sacred symbol, of Maman Brigitte, the Voudoun loa of the dead and protector of women. Or the aphorisms that constitute the last section, 'MOSAIC', explained as a ventriloquism from the sun when Reines was in a state of heightened receptivity following an intense rehearsal in New York, October 2014:

> ...entering me through the part of my head I sometimes call "my antenna," where my first white hairs grow, where my hair fell out while my mother was incarcerated on Riker's Island, & where, when a truck drove into me near Leogane, Haiti in 2010 I developed a bump, even though by all accounts it seemed I should have died.

The rangy scope of Reines' poetic concerns could be partly a function of her multi-hyphenate practice – poet, performance artist, playwright, translator, teacher and, curiously, astrologer offering a service called the 'Marguerite Hardass Birth Chart Reading', named for the French novelist Marguerite Duras. Other cultural references abound:

> I had studied the Dust Bowl, the architecture at Delphi, Judaic & Islamic legends of Moses, Midianite theology, the History of Haiti, Aryan horseman of ancient Iran, the collapse of Sumerian agriculture, Kundalini yoga, Allan Savory's & competing theories on desertification reversal, ancient contemporary methods of ruminant grazing, grasslands & myths of grasslands, those Hopi stories that can be found in books, Roman haruspicy, Hellenistic astrology, the life of the Marquis de Sade, one or two novels, one or two volumes of poetry, Bulgarian choral singing, elements of contemporary sculpture, certain Gnostic scriptures, my own appetite

And despite playing fast and loose with channelling Baudelaire, Baldwin, Spiegelman, Carson, Shakespeare, Mallarmé, Greek and Norse mythology, the poet despairs that "there are things not found in books / or perhaps you have been reading the wrong ones" and that it's "the selfsame / Vicious culture that drove us to retreat into the jail of our own / bones".

Perhaps calling this book a poetry collection is a misnomer. It's actually a soothsaying, syncretic ferment of grief, love, ecstasy, depression, infatuation, self-loathing, sex, humour, geography, women and their bodies, sex, climate change, violence, trauma, birds, the sun, the occult, the internet, celebrity culture, more sex and yes, sand. The ruinous spectre of sand is everywhere. It's in the titles of poems like 'Silicosis' and 'Haboob'. It pops up in names like George Sand, Bernie Sanders, Sandy Hook, Hurricane Sandy and Sandra Bland (the poet's mother's name is also Sandra), extending the metaphor of desertification into the trauma caused by spiritual moribundity. There are literal dust storms on Mars and figurative ones elsewhere. Just as sand is the erosion of rocks from weathering over millions of years, sand is figuratively connected to the tragedy and violence that has contributed to the attrition of the human soul over millennia.

The title and opening epigraph – "NO MORE SAND ART, no sand book, no masters" – are taken from a poem by Paul Celan. Like Celan, Reines' visionary and confessional poetics are concerned with the impossibility of faith and irreducibility of language. This refusal, and urgency to transcend the limits of language, sees the poet struggling against the collapse of hope brought on by the traumas of dislocation, alienation and exile caused by "something strange, something physical, gravel rattling over a burning plate in the belly, corrosive dread like frothing and seething, a fecal feeling, a dead feeling." In desperation the speaker of 'The Saddest Year of My Life' finds herself "crouching crouching over [her] phone / waiting for it to tell [her] what to do."

For all its apocalyptically epic grief, *A Sand Book* isn't devoid of humour. In 'Hegeling Before the Glass', for example, Reines writes about the "logic of the world robbing you of your boner". Ultimately, *A Sand Book* proves that Reines is a divining rod for our desiccated era.

. . .

Carolyn Forché's long-awaited new poetry collection *In the Lateness of the World* could also be said to begin with an intimation of sand, in its pre-weathered state as rocks, with the first poem 'Museum of Stones': "stone of cromlech and cairn, schist and shale, hornblende, / agate, marble, millstones, ruins of choirs and shipyards, / chalk, marl, mudstone from temples and tombs". This kind of listing, rich in nuanced detail, is typical of almost every poem in this slender collection. On its own this wouldn't be so remarkable. In combination with the long, loping lines that hardly vary from poem to poem, it becomes repetitive, highlighting Forché's limited poetic range. Conversely, it's in the rare moments when the poet turns her poetic gaze on herself such as in 'Travel Papers', or the last poem 'What Comes', that description crystallises into something that reaches beyond merely recreating moments in time reportage-style.

When Forché received the Hiroshima Foundation Award in 1998 following the publication of her second collection, *The Country Between Us*, which recounted her experiences in El Salvador just before the civil war, it was given to her for using her poetry as a "means to attain understanding, reconciliation, and peace within communities". That collection's distinguishing poem, 'The Colonel', distilled Forché's El Salvadoran experience so powerfully into meaning that it has come to define what the reader expects a Forché poem to be. This is unfair pressure given that it's been nearly two decades since Forché's last collection, but it's an unavoidable filter through which to consider her subsequent work.

In the past, Forché's oeuvre has been distinguished by her ability to merge political and personal concerns, but the personal is largely absent in this collection. Forché has said, "if we give up the dimension of the personal, we risk relinquishing one of the most powerful sites of resistance. The celebration of the personal, however, can indicate a myopia, an inability to see how larger structures of the economy and the state circumscribe, if not determine, the fragile realm of the individual." It is possible to over-correct in the opposite direction because the specifically personal can so often elucidate the abstract universal. The 41 poems in this collection are so divorced from the personal, that for all its descriptive power, the poetry can often seem translucent or ghostly. These are end times and many of the poems are elegies, so perhaps this is a deliberate poetic strategy. 'The Ghost in Heaven' and 'Ashes to Guazapa', for example, are dedicated to Leonel Gómez Vides, who first opened Forché's eyes to the political potential of poetry in El Salvador. Recalling his guidance in her memoir *What You Have Heard Is True* (2019), Forché writes, "It was as if he had stood me squarely before the world, removed the blindfold, and ordered me to open my eyes." While the blindfold hasn't exactly returned, it sometimes feel like we are reading these poems through gauze.

All this has the effect of making the title of the recent book, taken from a Robert Duncan poem, 'Poetry, a Natural Thing', feel like it promises more than it delivers. Forché certainly knows the limits of a 'poetry of witness' and acknowledges the futility of her self-appointed task. 'In Elegy for an Unknown Poet', she concludes "I am your translator. Pity me. It is impossible to slip ein Fremder into the mouth of another."

Dzifa Benson is a poet and dramatist who writes about poetry for various publications.

POETRY'S CUCKOOS

Sam Riviere, After Fame, *Faber, £10.99, ISBN 9780571356928*
Matthew Welton, SQUID SQUAD, *Carcanet, £10.99, ISBN 9781784109356*

Edwina Attlee on gestures, flexes and proofreaders' nightmares

. . .

The first time I read a poem by Sam Riviere it was on a little slip of good quality paper that had been dropped with hundreds of other fragments of poetry by a helicopter hovering over London's Southbank. It fell from the sky into my hand. My fragment was a brief recitation of all the prizes the poet had won – they were listed along with some grants, itemising how much money they consisted of. I must have been disappointed then, by the lack of poetry in my hands. In my memory, the people around me had clutched at the sky and come back with fists full of Neruda – fragments of heartache and metaphor. I was holding something that seemed to call into question the bounds of poetry, and that certainly prodded at the apparatus of its dissemination and production.

This collection, described as the final in the "loose trilogy" of Riviere's "process-derived" works, is doing the same thing, drawing attention with vertiginous self-consciousness to the structures that make and maintain that thing we call 'a poet': "These poems are designed to ingratiate their author within a particular system of expectation and reward" ('A Slave

Reader'). He does this, ostensibly, by writing versions of 118 epigrams by the Roman poet Martial. I have to take Riviere and Faber's word about Martial – my internet is down so I can't look him up, and maybe that's fine. The pre-existing parcels of text, written thousands of years in the past are not exactly irrelevant, they are a formal constraint, chanced upon when the poet was googling a number, followed like a clue or a sign from the gods. The move to follow a clue in the Googlescape is Oulipian, and *After Fame* sits comfortably in this canon and is similarly perverse, guarded, loose, experimental and nonsensical.

It's post-internet, in the sense described by Charles Whalley in this magazine in 2015 – meaning that the text depends upon collaboration between internet and poet. There are fruitful comparisons to be made between Riviere and Ben Lerner. Both make conceptually driven, formally political literature, but what makes the experience of reading them similar is their uncanny ability to focus in on the seemingly irrelevant technological detail. Epigram 117, apparently the description of a pre-production computer game called *Irretrievable*, is also a historical document. The two-page text is a cool account of that panicked but purposeful set of actions that make up searching for something online and in the various compartments of a computer. What's captured here is the way people who do not have real fluency in them, use these files and servers. There is so much guesswork and trial, and so much following instruction. Here the user clicks "without reading the description properly", skim reads, receives, follows, retreats, copies and pastes, slows down, is advised to reload. They encounter "trustworthy-looking" zip files. In James Joyce's *Ulysses* we see Leopold Bloom feeling in the inside of his hat rim, to see if there is something there. The gesture of feeling for something you can't see is important to the collection, as is Riviere's gesture of recording it. The diverse levels of literacy and modes of reading involved in contemporary texts (which include ante-linguistic web use) are referenced and deployed throughout. Writing about the Norwegian poet Auden Mortensen, Riviere describes an "iPhone note-to-self quality" about his work – the self-referential (subtweet-esque?) quality of the epigram is plundered here too, in a sustained involvement with the different registers of self-consciousness.

In Lerner's *The Topeka School* (2019) there is a character who does experiments on language loss – moments where because of illness or temporary incapacity people lose the ability to express themselves and to be understood. Lerner attunes his readers to the potential poetry of this kind of drivel and to the confusing mesmerising nothingness it can contain. Another character is a championship debater and is practised at the art of "the spread", stretches of linguistic virtuosity where nothing is said, but in such a way as to dazzle or bamboozle your opponent. The manipulation of speech to control or influence an audience makes someone an "agent", a figure predicted by Raymond Williams in *Culture and Society* (1958): "Any practical denial of the relation between conviction and communication, between experience and expression, is morally damaging alike to the individual and to the common language." This idea, of the mutually vulnerable individual and the language they speak and hear, is of vital importance to Lerner and Riviere, though Riviere's concern with morality is less explicit. He tests the ground between conviction and communication, and seems content to let the experiment fail, citing statistical machine translation, the process by which Google Translate 'learns' languages other than English: "the more a phrase is found in the vast corpora of text available, the more it will be offered as a translation" (Epigram 76). The system's constant improvement means Riviere will have less to work with, he wants the approximate, ("adequate") near-drivel that the machine gives him – "a process rich with pathos and ruinous comedy, indicating both the lossy edges of internet imperialism and the irretrievable distance of the source text" (76). Martial clearly writes in a disingenuous 'voice', but he is a good agent, because doing this within the space of a poem demonstrates a certain respect for his readers. Williams tells us, "Communication is not only transmission; it is also reception and response". *After Fame* sets up camp in that secondary zone.

The obvious point of contact between *After Fame* and *SQUID SQUAD* is Epigram 77, which is the length of two pages:

> Spins plates, still pale.
> Collects petals, still pale.
> Less ill, still pale.
> Il s'appelle, still pale.

Matthew Welton's fourth book begins with 64 flexes on four verses of alliterative, internally rhymed madness. The entire book is a proofreader's nightmare, and a cruel English teacher's dream ("class, identify and itemise the forms of rhyme deployed in *SQUID SQUAD*…").

> As she walks in a widening circle, Lola
> Wheeler leaves a spiral of footprints in the
> snow. Bradley Ridley feeds the chickens the
> chestnuts. Natalie Chatterly drums on an
> upturned bucket.
>
> (25)

In the forty-ninth of these flexes, we read "that language is what we're left with when we're through with communication". These verses are true to this writing position – delivering or transmitting not much by way of story or sense, but leaving the reader with the meaty leftovers of language; the bits that get stuck in your listening teeth. As I was reading I kept seeing the image of a large piece of farming equipment, from a satellite's perspective, making great sweeps through patchworks of field (as happens in Marco Cadioli's photographs). I think this is because of their involving musicality, they seem to move through you, and to move through you as a body – you want to say these words out loud, they twist your tongue.

Saying something out loud is one of the themes of the series – there is a playful tension between thought and speech, and between action and the miming of action. In the series characters mime the action of:

> rocking a baby
> buttering toast
> dialling a number
> popping a cork
> reeling in a fish
> sawing a log
> juggling with eggs
> unpeeling a banana
> grinding pepper
> focussing a pair of binoculars

To mime is to act without words or props. These mimed gestures are made up of a verb directed at or to a noun. They take the reader in two directions, the first is the acute sense of linguistic foolishness that Welton is attuned to; he plays with and sends up a series of literary conventions, including those of criticism. You are kept on your toes by a poet who has his characters mutter, "Any metaphor is a metaphor for the idea of metaphor", or think to themselves, "Knowing knowing gets us nowhere gets us nowhere" (25). In this context to write about something is only ever to mime an action, to grind the pepper of received experiences, to mimic rather than create, copying instead of transforming. And yet, how beautiful a series of actions! I would dearly like to see a danced performance of these poems.

The mimes are also a reason to stop reading and to start imagining, or to imagine in another way. The poems seem to interrupt themselves, leading the reader out of their reading. Like Riviere, Welton is a poet who resists the idea of a stable, complete, consumable poem, as his iterative patterns of poems (in a book that calls itself "a novel") show – and certainly, both books are short on satisfaction, questioning in different ways what poetic satisfaction might be. The mimed actions, like unoriginal incorrect versions of ancient epigrams, seem to take us to the brink of textual meaning, again and again, and then leave us there, like cartoon coyotes, scrabbling in midair.

Edwina Attlee's pamphlet the cream *was published by clinic in 2016.*

ROOTS THAT GRASP THE SKY

Bhanu Kapil, How To Wash A Heart, *Pavilion, £9.99,*
ISBN 9781789621686
Samira Negrouche, The Olive Trees' Jazz and Other Poems,
trans. Marilyn Hacker, Pleiades, $17.95, *ISBN 9780997099454*

Khairani Barokka on outer and inner worlds, freedom and entrapment

. . .

One book is a wind's-eye view of homes; the other, a record of growing anxiety, gusting inside oneself in unsafe houses. *The Olive Trees' Jazz and Other Poems*, by Samira Negrouche, translated by Marilyn Hacker, and *How To Wash A Heart*, Bhanu Kapil's long-awaited first collection published in the UK, are narrations of space, home, confinement, freedom, entrapment and escape – what they do to our hearts and our bodies, what they do to our selves.

There is a sense of entering distinct spaces when one reads these, a venturing into different spatial awarenesses as prescribed by narrators' voices. Kapil writes from the perspective of a house guest, increasingly cognisant of their host's power to hurt them, as analogy for racialised minorities in white-majority countries. Negrouche, on the other hand, writes of external and internal landscapes, abstract and lyrical. There is relief and catharsis from both writers, even as harshness permeates, for this harshness is a reflection of our violence-filled days. There are the narrators' deceptively calm voices in the face of storms.

In Kapil's book, the storm is one that has raged for so very long, and continues to. It is immersed in the experience we racialised as minorities in Western countries – including migrants, and their descendants – feel so sharply that we must find ways to dull it day to day. A cage, an encasement of freedom, which may seem imperceptible, but are, but are, but are. Negrouche's work, on the other hand, is free of captivity. Flies from seashore to seashore. Both books declare their presence forcefully, the narrators' singular voices as pulsing bloodstreams. Both offer verse that is sharp and tender, powerful and nimble.

An Algiers-born writer, translator, and doctor, Negrouche writes prose poems which are powerful flows of wind. Each a separate air journey, from "the rock paintings / of Tassili" to "the cradle / of a / wireless network" ('Six makeshift trees around my bathtub'), straddling seas. As Hacker writes in her introduction, she has "a sometimes conversational tone, and an enigmatic one that borders the surreal". Negrouche's verse is both liminal and intractable.

The narrator's voice lives "in the flexible moment / of a time that will not settle" ('While you pass by'), and the immediacy and lived experience of "that still- / burning skin / the rhythm / that rises" ('Only the electric pole'). The reader finds oneself taken on a ship of stanzas from one point to another, to another, a to-and-fro that is spelled out in how her lines "go and go and come / in oscillating rhythm, / of the aquatic   neck / seismic pulse-beat" ('Variations on a minor third').

It is a testament to the poet's skill, in concentrating descriptions of both emotion and landscape to form the whole, that scattered geographically here does not mean inconsequential or thoughtless. In fact, the writing evokes the very opposite – in the wisdom of showing us how multifarious life is, nature is, emotions are, letting us be in the flow where the outer world is the inner world: there is in one poem the idea of "lowering the sails and loving you without restraint" ('To invent the word?').

> Uncoiling
> of sea stars
> goddesses' nuptials of O
> Olympia of aural velvet
> opened to these fingers

roots
that grasp the sky

('Variations on a minor third')

The physical world is at one with groundedness and the self. The ocean is an anchoring force, with its repeated appearances throughout, "to leave and return / in the recaptured flow of the sea" ('The Olive Trees' Jazz'). The sea that has framed civilisations, built trade winds of history.

And what is so affirming, so lovable about these collected works of new and old verse by Negrouche, is how her work is, in Hacker's words, "both located in its origins and blissfully oblivious of national or any other borders". A truer rendering of how life is, how it should be held and written, without adhering to the fictions of empires built on arbitrary carvings of a map. The voice here in these poems is a map. Non-linear, unpredictable, descriptive in ways that feel wholly new.

I particularly adored the prose poems in 'Seven Jasmine Monologues', with its sections named after cities, evoking them in landscapes felt from the inside out: Rabat, Algiers, Damascus, Sanaa, Cairo, Tripoli, Tunis. A woman gives "my *djilbab-string* to the sea", a speaker addresses a "Holy Man" of Damascus, whose followers are persecuted.

> Holy man in your land souls left the wall's shadow and surged up as One their burgeoning shadows were arrested and they remained One their eyelashes were broken their gaze smothered and they remained One.

The "you" in Negrouche's writings is a diverse one, speaking to lover, speaking to anointed spiritual figure, speaking to the places these voices evoke as equals in nature. This is in contrast to the cutting "you" in Kapil's collection, which often addresses its white host in heart-rending monologues, the walls of a house as threatening container. While both books defy borders and control, the latter is distinctly held captive to them, by them, within them – brutal sectioning of peoples and lands past and present, Partition, ethnonationalism. The world we were born into.

How To Wash A Heart's poems, without titles, presented as a unified totality of experience, follow an arc from gratitude and trust to scenes of growing terror, crescendoing.

In her afterword, Kapil writes

This is the voice of this book: an immigrant guest in the home of their citizen host.

The speaker is an artist.

The red and the heart and the ice speak through them.

A performance artist herself, one who weaves ritual through altars, Kapil as a leader of ceremony takes us through unsafe terrain. The pages, marked by displays of affection (sexual, motherly, platonic) and hospitality from a "host" we may read as white, sharply draw nonetheless familiar aggressions, still dismissed by many as small. Indicative of deep-seated hatreds and historical infliction of traumas, from those who, like the narrator's host, may have adopted a daughter, an "'Asian refugee' / As you described her". And who, like the narrator's host, may end up literally sacrificing host and daughter, may well present home and place as altar of a kind not liable to tenderly cleanse a heart. Always threatening action, a blow.

My spiritual power was quickly depleted
By living with you.
Like an intrusive mother, you cared for my needs
But also, I never knew
When you might open my door, leaving it open
When you left.

In captivity, the tactics of survival are of concealment and calculation.

I understood that you were a wolf
Capable of devouring
My internal organs
If I exposed them to view.
Sure enough, the image of a heart
Carved from the body
Appeared
In the next poem you wrote.

It is profoundly felt, how Kapil delves into the subtleties of living with acute fear for one's safety, of being forced to represent, and reflect, one's host's ideas of vast histories: "I don't want to beautify our collective trauma. [...] // As your guest, I trained myself / To beautify / Our collective trauma." In life, as in art.

Heart in throat, we feel the creative power of the guest versus – directly and actively versus – the creative power of the host. The narrator resisting, and evoking too easily (particularly for those of us who survive it daily), the violence of academia, and cultural spaces, and all spaces in such conditions of inequity. As places of performative allyship, enacted by all those most benefiting from white supremacy towards those whom white supremacy inflicts its wounds upon.

> Verbally, you state egalitarian
> Ideals.
> Financially, you hook
> That brown baby
> Up.

And also as places where solidarity among similarly racialised subjects is seen as aggressive and is open to sabotage:

> Your daughter and I smiled, buzzing [...]
> That night, you refused to say a word
> To either of us.
> Is silence an axe
> Raised above the head?

The searing end of the book is culmination and manifestation, of the real and present danger the host has always presented to the narrator. It is immediately reminiscent of the fire and repatriation in the UK's treatment of immigrant families, Grenfell and Windrush; daughter and guest both in pain.

This work is to be cherished for its honesty. A sense of relief gifted to readers that yes, this is life. One shall not be gaslit. One's heart is a thing to protect.

The similarities between Kapil's and Negrouche's works lie in the way the verse-wind winds around what it perceives, maintaining an "i"-ness throughout liminal landscapes. The internal fleshing out our world from the inside, as it always does, in such striking and disparate ways.

These books are gems. Both authoritative in the best sense of the word; stridently reflecting worlds of their own – that we know, and yet have never read described in this particular way, according to the contours along which our hearts move. The grooves of everyday architectures; sea, winds, houses, veins.

Khairani Barokka is Associate Artist at the National Centre for Writing, and Researcher-in-Residence at UAL's Decolonising Arts Institute.

A POCKET BABEL

Ranjit Hoskote, The Atlas of Lost Beliefs, *Arc, £11.99,*
ISBN 9781911469636
Roger Robinson, A Portable Paradise, *Peepal Tree, £9.99,*
ISBN 9781845234331

Marek Sullivan on borders, context and accountability

. . .

Ranjit Hoskote's *The Atlas of Lost Beliefs* (2020) is an epic in three parts, the culmination of "a twenty-year-long project of research and translation", as the biographical note states, which draws together dazzling meditations on history, language, colonialism, Herman Melville, Upanishadic philosophy, Vedic theology, art and the ocean. According to James Byrne, Hoskote "reappropriates the love poem" and there is certainly romance here, from the "scattershot" rain that "pelts" Hoskote's skin while he sits astride a scooter at a light ('Poona Traffic Shots') to the deep longing of a body "denied / two yards of spaded earth in the Loved One's country" ('The Heart Fixes on Nothing').

A strong vein of Indian postcolonial theory crosses the collection. Many of the poems can be seen as a direct extension of the vigorous debates around language and imperialism advanced by Gayatri Spivak, Homi Bhabha and Ania Loomba during the 1980s and '90s. Finding their ideas brought to life several decades later in language that fizzes with invention is a strange experience, already coloured by nostalgia and in that sense historical. In another collection this might have seemed passé but Hoskote breathes life into old ideas, riffing with abandon on the organicity of lost or endangered tongues (Konkani, Tulu, Sabir, etc) against the rigidifying power of modern languages and their intimate relation to state formations. In 'The Map Seller', a kind of grand tour of the world in 100 empires, Hoskote pictures himself peddling maps like ice-creams: "Whatever you like, I've got a map that looks like it – / and you can have any piece of my flaking jigsaw atlas". The atlas may be flaking but the border lines are real. They are re-erected and reinscribed as we read, buttressed by new promises in old wine skins: "And across this trench that a JCB's dug along my street: / tomorrow's avenue, today's wide sludge grave."

If dug earth divides past from future, one state and the next, the ocean tends to erase boundaries and dance upon them, like the blue-handed "reckless dancer" who "poses, heels in the air, Cossack-kicking on a crumbling reef" ('The Atlas of Lost Beliefs'). There is no time for hubris here, or rather, there is too much time:

> my name is Ocean
>   I shall not be contained
>   my tides spell
>   starting gun and finish line
> afterwards only shells
>   and scattered roofs
> will remind you I was
>   there
>   ('Ocean')

Where borders appear in water, they are dangerous, exposed places subject to unpredictable fluctuations that disrupt the lattice of language. Sharks drift at the boundary line ("this is the jolt where nerve end meets salt, / this is the neverskin, / this is where you grow knife-edged fins and plunge" – 'Cape Caution'). In a poem based on a copper engraving by hydrographers in the East India Company, language snaps where "The river stabs the sea". Here, "the coast signals its own tongue: // breaking with the horizon's grammar, / a stutterance" ('As It Emptieth It Selfe'). River, sea, coast – three solid words describing unsolid things. How has the nation state survived reality for so long? Hoskote reminds us that state integrity will always be accompanied by paranoia, nightmares of linguistic and racial miscegenation or what the anthropologist Mary Douglas memorably called "matter out of place".

Despite its propensity for linguistic proliferations, *The Atlas of Lost Beliefs* is not interested in suspending univocality for its own sake. Hoskote's scepticism about language and identity is, rather, the starting point for a deeper search, one rooted in love, beauty and art. In 'A Constantly Unfinished Instrument', dedicated to Brian Eno, the author evokes the thrilling search for aesthetic form with a synthesiser, a device that is unencumbered by the baggage of tradition and uniquely requires musicians to generate both instrument and sound in a single gesture. Unmoored from the structuring weight of the past, Eno casts off in search of musical beauty like a Captain Ahab of the sonorous: "Stay the course until you've caught / the quick, true surge of the ocean / that's felt the fire harpoon pierce its side". Yet despite the chaos and contingency of the pursuit, there is a sense here of an order to be found and pinned down. The poem ends "heard it right".

Hoskote's resistance to anomie is perhaps the most romantic aspect of *The Atlas of Lost Beliefs*. The linguistic and cultural homogeneity of modern nations may spell the death of cultures and beliefs but the nightmare of a horizon wiped clean by difference is just as intolerable. The poem 'Under the Tree of Tongues' consists of the single line, "there is no healing." Such nods to prelapsarian unity are, however, constantly offset by Hoskote's own scepticism about language – particularly the language of the coloniser in which he is compelled to write: "Lord of lost perspectives, / this might be the wrong prayer: / Give me back the untroubled pleasures / of the sovereign eye" ('Baldachin'). Even as Hoskote yearns for a time before Babel he also casts doubt on the validity of that search, since "this might be the wrong prayer". The question is, how would we know?

. . .

A Portable Paradise (2019) was the winner of last year's T.S. Eliot Prize, catapulting Roger Robinson into the limelight after decades of work supporting young talent from the sidelines. Robinson is a co-founder of the London poetry collective Malika's Poetry Kitchen, and until 2000 he coordinated the performance poetry organisation Apples and Snakes. The language of the collection is straightforward, unflourished, often didactic.

There is a resistance to streamlining and sophistication, and some of the best poems are simply-told stories from the fringes. The collection opens with an elegy for the victims of Grenfell, in which the smoke of the fire mingles metaphorically with spirits of the Day of Judgement. At the beginning, the "Risen" float into the air from "front pews", while at the end

> A hundred people start floating
> from the windows of a tower block;
> from far enough away they could be
> black smoke from spreading flames
> ('The Missing')

The circumlocutory "from far enough away they could be" is characteristic of the whole collection. Sometimes the circumlocution works, sometimes it seems like an editorial oversight. Here, I read the phrase as a necessary hinge between speculation and reality. Robinson's dark image of reckoning is an inversion of the poeticising eye that would callously allegorise the black smoke of Grenfell into an abstract eschatological event. The unusual order of the simile (spirit before materiality) combined with the oblique "they could be" suggests, among other things, that the horror of Grenfell may be harder to accept than Christ's second coming.

Deliberate circumlocution aside, the collection contains several apparent mistakes. One poem ('Haibun for the Lookers') contains a repetition of "charred", first in the line "their orange floral / wallpaper slowly bubbling up and bursting like blisters before giving / in to a blackened charred heat", then again a few lines down, in "The building has become a charred black tomb". There seems to be no justification for this repetition, and one gets the sense – rightly or wrongly – that Robinson just liked the word. It appears again, three pages later, in 'Blame': "survivors walk like zombies / trying not to look up / at the charred gravestone." An editor might also have pointed out that there is no need for the simile "bursting like blisters", since 'blistering' is conventionally used to describe that phenomenon. This type of error – and I would argue it is unambiguously an error – accumulates throughout the collection, from the unnecessary adverb in "finches darting / deftly between [the Risen]" ('The Missing') to the pat simile in "Sweat dripping / off his face like tears" ('(Some) Sweat').

These are elementary problems of composition and yet there are other, more fundamental problems, too, namely a surprising lack of political, racial and economic context to Grenfell and Windrush, bar the history of slavery. This issue is especially acute in the poem 'Dolls', where Robinson recapitulates the series of factors that led to Grenfell by stating what he wished had happened differently, beginning with the *Daily Mail*'s favourite ground zero, "Muhammed's fridge that exploded and started the fire". Robinson writes, "I would give Muhammed some clue that all was not right with it", then runs through the gamut of alternative events – he wishes that families were out of the building, that the children were visiting their grandparents, etc. Any blame for political or other structural failings is condensed into the final line: "I'd make the cladding that burned like straw be fireproofed to international standards". The same theme pops up halfway through the collection, this time treated with anger, in 'Citizen II': "How is it I'm begging you for housing, / when you burnt my building down?" But who is the "you" if Muhammed's fridge was part of the problem? How do political and natural accountability intersect? Robinson seems to be railing against two adversaries, the racist state and the universe, the second of which encompasses the first and cannot be beaten.

Male sexuality and the sexualisation of blackness thread through several poems. In 'Black Anthurium', Robinson sets the "priapic" titular plant with "deep black gleaming skin" against the historical fact that "convicted / white French women / [...] were given a choice: have sex / with the strongest black slave / and bear a child into slavery, / or be imprisoned for life back in France." Both Black Anthuriums and the descendants of slavery are "The legacy of genetic breeding" and both must "adapt to new environments" and "produce new flowers". Robinson's play on the literal sexualisation of black men and the rape of women by the state is a great piece of historical excavation and could have formed the basis for the entire collection. As it is, the idea is slightly buried within a cluster of sub-themes that can't help but dilute the poem's power.

In an interview for *The Guardian* Robinson observes that "There's a reason people are acting out – the pressure and despair of trying to survive. People shouldn't divorce the behaviour from the context causing it. It's a traumatic time." Reading *A Portable Paradise*, I sought more of this context, more depth of analysis, more history and more consistency.

Marek Sullivan is a joiner and writer based in Bristol, UK.

THE WOUND AND ITS REMEDY

David Morley, FURY, *Carcanet, £10.99,* *ISBN 9781784109905*
Natalie Diaz, Postcolonial Love Poem, *Faber, £10.99,*
ISBN 9780571359868

Zakia Carpenter-Hall on spells of creation and pathways to enlightenment

. . .

To be a poet, and a speaker of any language, is to be like a lyrebird: it's to compose your 'song' from sounds you've heard before, but to combine those melodies distinctly and uniquely so that their specific arrangement is only identifiable as you.

David Morley's seventh collection contains seven "lyrebird" poems which all possess such showmanship and sonic agility, as well as the kind of posturing and braggadocio characteristic of the boxer Tyson Fury after whom the collection is named.

Structurally, each lyrebird poem has the alternating anaphora "My vow" and "Your vow", suggesting a code of ethics and honour, even if the full nature of the vow is unspoken:

> My vow yawns the dawn chorus's enormous Yes.
> My vow will never master the art of loss.

> Your vow condenses Stratus, Cirrus, and Altocumulus.
> Your vow sees worlds in grains of sand, heavens in wildflowers.
> ('Third Lyrebird')

These vows are active; they precipitate, yawn, condense, see, court. Like social norms and cultural practices, the vows Morley writes about hint at a code that's rarely – if ever – explicitly stated, but forms the customs by which people live. They also signify a pact with the reader. They are evidence that the reader enters into an agreement with the author once she begins reading a text. In this sense, every poem is a kind of vow, promise or agreement.

Morley's first promise to the reader is one of verbal versatility and imitation. In the first line of 'First Lyrebird' the speaker states, "Your vow is the Lyrebird's thesaurus of mimicry". 'Seventh Lyrebird' ends with an almost identical line, except that it opens with "My vow" instead of "Your vow". The pronouns "You" and "My" seem interchangeable and are early indications of circular and reflexive syntaxes that Morley uses throughout the collection. He seeks to dazzle and include the audience in his cyclical song, his thesaurus of words, his mimicry.

The syntax wraps around subjects in a kind of linguistic spiral, recalling poems like Kathleen Raine's 'A Spell for Creation' and Ted Hughes's 'Amulet', which use anaphora and anadiplosis. The beginning of 'Amulet' reads: "Inside the Wolf's fang, the mountain of heather. / Inside the mountain of heather, the Wolf's fur" and continues until the poem eventually returns and ends with "the Wolf's fang". Morley references 'Amulet' by using similar terms in 'The Thrown Voice', ie "mountain of error", "heather", "lone fir", and writes his own spell of creation:

> Those wound, wounded voices were thrown
> into me, as if bird and tree were hornbooks
> I could finger and trace and sing aloud.
> I spoke through night, or night through me
> and all the creatures of the night sang free.
> My Gypsies gave tongue to campfire stories
> but my spell drew speech from the circling heath.
> I was a magician to them, the magic man
> to my people. I lost it. I lost my magic
> when I lost those voices. I cried my eyes out.

> I have cried my eyes into myself. How can
> you know what it is like to lose your magic?

The source of the magician's magic and voice was "night which throws / her voice / inside a bird". Morley skilfully sets up the logic of his collection – the logic of someone who had a childhood stammer – that the words we speak originate someplace beyond us, a "thrown voice". Not only is language cyclical and borrowed, to speak is a kind of ventriloquism.

If the source of one's voice is beyond the speaker, it belongs to both no one and everyone. The voice can, according to this logic, be thrown or projected ever further. This is the rationale of the persona poems, the majority of this collection, which feature Romany English and experiences of Roma people, including Tyson Fury and Wisdom Smith's life and descendants, along with a modified ghazal in the voice of Yemeni Guantanamo Bay detainee Towfiq Bihani. Morley's poetics of mimicry and ventriloquism echo the collection's subjects of displaced peoples and species, illustrating the virtuosity of voice, in a mutually reinforcing loop.

...

"I know what it's like to be appetite of your own appetite, / citizen of what savages you, / to dare bloom pleasure from your wounds—", writes Natalie Diaz in 'I, Minotaur'. Both *FURY* and *Postcolonial Love Poem* maintain a reflexive relationship between the collections' central wound and remedy; the former's is voice, the latter's is the need for water.

Diaz uses the concept of "water memory", the idea that water retains traces of whatever it's encountered, to tell the story of "an indissoluble relationship with the world" ('*exhibits from* The American Water Museum'). Paradoxically, the need for water describes both the wound and its remedy. In the title poem, Diaz writes:

> The rain will eventually come, or not.
> Until then, we touch our bodies like wounds—
> the war never ended and somehow begins again.

War takes on various meanings in this collection, but perhaps the most prominent is the erasure of Native peoples and their interrelatedness with the landscape: erasing one erases both. This conflict is primarily depicted in the war for water; think of the encampment at Standing Rock.

Diaz's writing, concerned with winning on multiple fronts, suggests that one way to counteract the war of erasure is to become "better" at existing – more vivid, fully embodied and alive through shapeshifting and outmanoeuvring one's opponents:

> And we won by doing what all Indians before us had done against their bigger, whiter opponents—we became coyotes and rivers, and we ran faster [...] up and down the court, game after game. We became the weather—we blew by them, we rained buckets [...]
>
> [...] we pulled the trigger on jumpers all damn day.
>
> ('Run'n'Gun')

Though 'Run'n'Gun' is about basketball, it reveals this collection's essential feature: to always be on the verge of becoming. This slip and glide out of almost any grasp is how the collection emulates its central motif that flows in the bodies of Mojave people: the Colorado River. Aliveness, like a river's current, means constantly changing. In '*exhibits from* The American Water Museum', Diaz writes, "The water piped into every American city is called *dead water.*" Death implies the loss of spontaneity and agency. You don't win – and you definitely don't survive – by being static.

Diaz provides glimpses of Mojave and Diné origin stories intertwined with the biblical Eden reimagined. She emphasises ascension rather than "the fall", and immanence rather than transcendence. The following passage could be likened to tasting the fruit of knowledge:

> *What's in your love's eyes?* I tell them. Wild sugar-
> melons, green-on-green, on green. She and I,
> we eat the melons, starting at their thick-syruped
> hearts, hold the beady seeds in our mouths
> like new eyes, wait for them to leap open
> and see us first.
>
> ('Like Church')

In the Bible, eating the forbidden fruit and the resulting knowledge brings the fall of mankind. In Diaz's garden, eating the fruit is a divine communion and awakening. Desire for a feminine lover who is inseparable from the landscape occurs throughout this collection. Diaz explains to the reader in 'The First Water Is The Body', "Unless you know the context of a conversation, you might not know if we are speaking about our body or our land [...] You might not know we mean both." She uses this Mojave confluence among personhood-water-land-divinity throughout the collection – offering a radical interpretation of 1 Corinthians 11:24,"Take, eat, this is My body which is broken for you..."

And sometimes wounding provides a pathway to enlightenment:

> My brother now wants to give me the knife.
> Some might say, *My brother wants to stab me.*
>
> He tries to pass it to me—like it is a good thing.
> Like, *Don't you want a little light in your belly?*
>
> Like the way Orion and Scorpius—
> across all that black night—pass the sun.
> ('Blood-Light')

Diaz uses fable, ecstatic poetry, prose to "wage love and worse" ('Postcolonial Love Poem'), urging readers to realise our "indissoluble relationship with the world". Here the English language restricts us, for what we're also discussing is Water as an entity worthy of personhood rights. In 'The First Water Is the Body', she writes, "If I could convince you, would our brown bodies and our blue rivers be more loved and less ruined?"

Zakia Carpenter-Hall's poetry reviews and essays have also been published by Poetry London, *The Poetry School and* Wild Court.

DREAMS

Caleb Femi, Poor, *Penguin, £9.99,* ISBN 9780141992150
Rachel Long, My Darling from the Lions, *Picador, £10.99,*
ISBN 9781529045161

Stephanie Sy-Quia on two impactful debuts

. . .

In Caleb Femi's *Poor*, the second-person pronoun is deployed in an implicatory capacity, in the manner of Claudia Rankine's *Citizen* (2014). "I have nothing to offer you / but my only pair of Nike Air Max 90s", begins 'Concrete (I)', reaching us in the voice of a young dead black man, and his "you" leaves the reader unabsolved of the forces that have caused his death:

> Take with them
> God's speed through the valley of days
> low yielding in laughs when the grey of
> the concrete is louder than your outfit.

The ending, when it comes, knocks you sideways: "and when you walk, walk proud, / for you walk in what I might have been". With its opening line, and considering the collection's title, the poem echoes Yeats's 'He wishes for the Cloths of Heaven' ("But I, being poor, have only my dreams; I have spread my dreams under your feet; / Tread softly because you tread on my dreams").

The imposed guilt of living "when better boys / deserved life" is a throughline in the collection, which centres on life on North Peckham Estate, a notorious so-called 'sink estate', and at one time one of the most deprived residential areas in Western Europe, since subject to massive regeneration efforts in the 1990s and 2000s. The architectural ambition of the blocks, with their Brutalist-inflected optimism and theories of modern living, receives some sharp attention. Questions abound about "all that hopeful good on powder-blue paper", and its materialisation into the site of "your blooming, your making-do", where young boys are "in search of a hyperbolic time chamber / where their clutch of years pours slow" ('Put them in the room of spirit and slow time'). In 'A Designer Talks of a Home / A Resident Talks of Home' (I & II), the designers' pretensions are slowly, stylishly eviscerated by splicing together what might be transcriptions: "00:20:15 *'cause concrete smells like a siege [...] when it rains I like to* // 00:04:23 imbue people with a sense of wellbeing, empowerment, gentle joyfulness." Meanwhile, living in the built environment so loftily imagined,

> Each dawn I wake and scroll myself for new scars,
> confess that I want to live for good times:
> picnic with a peng ting, lips her on the grass.
> But every day, on the endz, there is a procession
> my breathing body mocks.
>
> ('Survivor's Guilt, or Anikulapo')

In 'Trauma is a Warm Bath', we are told to

> Just ask the mother who worked
> until her hands curled like boiled crabs
> to have a son on safer shores; fed him;
> bought him toothpaste for two decades, almost

The demand recalls Ta-Nehisi Coates in his incantatory, nation-shaking *Between the World and Me* (2015), relaying the police murder of his friend – "Think of soccer balls, science kits, chemistry sets, racetracks, and model trains. Think of all [...] that had gone into him, sent flowing back to the earth." One hopes that Femi will have a similar impact. He writes with a grace and persistence which cannot, and will not, one hopes, be ignored.

Early on in Rachel Long's debut collection, *My Darling from the Lions*, we encounter a holiday argument between lovers: "You say / *I don't think I'll identify with a brown son*". It's the sort of high-stakes argument glossed over in alarmed hurry, because "We're eating roses on a rooftop. The Med beneath us", patched up with sex on a hotel balcony: "is love not this? – gripping a fence in the sky". Child-rearing, or the spectre thereof, forms a major theme of the collection. In 'Self-Portrait with Baby', an infant appears on a doorstep, "Curled cute as a prawn in her pink-brushed cotton", which brings us up short; "cute as a prawn" is a markedly odd image, but it perfectly captures the fundamental strangeness of children to those who feel their material circumstances may inhibit parenthood. In 'Portent', our speaker confesses:

> I feel middle class when I'm in love.
> I think it's all the poached eggs on bird-seed bread,
> staying up all night on Zoopla – imagine
> waking under cottage beams,
> the laughter in a garden. Kids.
> A little boy with gold hair
> keeps standing in my dreams.

The keenly observed class signifiers, meted out with mordant wit in pithy plosives, belie an earnest yearning, capped off with the sudden, caesural "Kids". Like the gold-haired little boy, children haunt this collection with the very potentiality of their presence, a presence hampered by a "hand-held shower" and "the gaffer-taped loo". In circumstances such as these, children themselves (with an implied whiteness: prawn-coloured baby, gold-haired boy) have become a potent sign standing at the nexus of middle-class poached eggs, gardens, and cottage beams. Through her chorus of speakers, Long writes searingly of these fraught desires, felt so keenly in the members of a younger generation dogged by low living standards and financial insecurity. Her poems, with their deft footwork between humour and longing, linger with one palimpsestically throughout the day.

Alongside these are poems about having been mothered, and the special freighting of mothering (or having been) a mixed-race child. This is manifest through the site of hair, such as the maternal labour of plaiting. "'Look at you, beautiful as Winnie Mandela!'", says the mother in 'Jail

Letter'. The unspoken retort is hilariously sharp and concise, speaking volumes about black histories and perceptions thereof: "I don't know who this is, / but it doesn't sound like someone Ben Clark would fancy". 'Communion' alludes to the chimera-like transformations of getting a weave ("Choose a new version of yourself / every 2–3 months. Be Russian, Hawaiian, / Virgin – at 8, 16, / 22 inches. Go electric blue, blonde"). Most poignantly, the poem's speaker asks, "Ever sat for thirteen hours / in the same chair?", your scalp wrenched and raked into someone else's punitive beauty ideal? Hair, lest we forget,

> ...is a crowning glory.
> A source not only of beauty but power.
> Remember Samson?
> It can be taken,
> buried in the woods at night.
> Everything you came into this world with,
> all you were to achieve,
> the love you were meant for,
> trodden, rotting under the earth.
> ('Mum's Snake')

Such is its significance, that as a child in 'Apples', the speaker dreams she is "The Most Beautiful Woman in the World":

> I had the best hair
> and even did humanitarian work.
> I was interviewed
> about both things,
> each night, for TV.

Long's use of humour to cloak more acute sentiment is fabulously stylish. It imparts a certain subversive joy to the reader, in the refusal to offer up painful experiences straightforwardly for our gaze, and offers a mode to other writers with similar things to share.

Stephanie Sy-Quia is a freelance writer based in London. She is currently working on her first book of poetry.

BIRDSONG AND DAYBREAK

Peter Gizzi, Sky Burial: New & Selected Poems, *Carcanet, £14.99,*
ISBN 9781784108229

Rachael Allen on prophecy, disruption and uncertainty

...

Sky Burial opens with the poet's newest and previously uncollected pieces. The book's first poem, 'Speech Acts for a Dying World', feels pertinent to the point of prophecy in its enforced and interrogated interiority, as communities around the world move between various states of being confined to the places that they live. The speaker, in an acknowledgement of the lineage of poets before them, is gazing out of a window, ruminating on what they see. A sparrow taps on this window, "trying to communicate", which instead of gifting the speaker a kind of pastoral or sublime realisation of the natural world, is instead an irritation: "getting to me". This springboard for the poem, the view from a window, opens into a theoretical and emotional treatise on looking out *while* looking in; the exhaustion of managing the relationship between external stimulation with subjective perspective. The poem, like much of Gizzi's work, is concerned with the tension between the felt possibilities and communicative responsibility of articulating ideas of truth, of what is both emotionally present and materially seen.

In poeticising this conundrum, the speaker's thinking becomes both restrained and frenetic, shifting and correcting itself within the speech. In the same poem, in-text contradictions and edits abound: "when I said work / and meant lyric", the world is "high-toned" and "shitty", while still being "inherited" and "phenomenal". In a line of thinking and poetics similar to Elizabeth Bishop's sequence of shifts and corrections (from 'The Map', "Shadows, or are they shallows?", and 'The Monument', "built somewhat like a box. No. Built / like several boxes"), subjectivity in these poems is queried and questioned through a ludic and self-reflexive notion of the self, as in 'Caption': "earlier I said landscape // How did it come about?", or the very Bishop-esque, "It thought the world was wide / Afterword said it was narrow" ('Ledger Domain').

This grappling with how we lean the external alongside ideas of interiority is at an emotional apex in another recent poem, 'From This End of Sadness', a text that feels sodden with grief:

> From this end
> of sadness
> there's nothing
> out there I want
> and wonder
> if there's anything
> in here I need?

Here, all of Gizzi's poetic traits come together to create a treatise on what it means to mourn. The conversational asides and colloquialisms that feature in many of his other poems, which feel particular to a specific American demotic in poetry, offer their easy frames to support intense, philosophical lines that are almost Möbius-strip-like in how they return a reader to themselves, ourselves, and the poem, and are never solved:

> I'm into the way
> the technology of an I
> is filled with the dead

Gizzi's seemingly easy "I", as in other poems, is tussled and wrestled with. This "I" is so many things. It is "coeval" with a "rotting trunk", it's also "into that medieval / light glancing / through leaves". This "I" tries to find a line in a day and does not understand the "code that held / me to the world".

Away from 'From This End of Sadness' – a poem that moves its text on the page as physically as grief moves through a body – Gizzi's wrought and elastic "I" is the uncertain but also deftly certain "eye" (or many "eyes") that these visionary lyrics stem from. Gizzi knows the work that an "I" does, and also how we must question what is accepted as seen, something written plainly in his gesturing to the expansiveness of this small pronoun as a "technology".

These pontifications on truth, the self and perspective are also evidenced in Gizzi's ludic syntax and playful stream of sometimes oblique metaphoric junctions, as in 'Caption', again: "Grief unlike truth, truth unlike snow / Body unlike its outline". This uneasy relationship between speaking and feeling what is truthful, or honest, is reflected in this unique syntax. Gizzi's experimentations with the sentence are evident in his older poems, and sometimes writ explicitly so, as in the earlier poem 'Ledger Domain', where command follows action: "Syntax bent the child / – playing on the page // Speech – be quiet!" This strange merging of concepts and speech patterns – a comment on the affect of language, the performed scolding one would give a child, the attention through punctuation ("!") – melds to give this comment on language a supple materiality. Is it the image of a child playing on the page that is "bent" for the reader by a disruption in syntactical sense? Or is the poem scolding itself for its play? The lines open up for us kaleidoscopically, generating new meaning and sense each way we choose to read them. Reading Gizzi's poetry feels close to thinking, a representation of the mind and its capriciousness.

The generosity and openness in Gizzi's poetry extends beyond theme and form. Inside his poems you hear echoes of many different schools of American poetry. There are the louche, conversational and emotive tones of the New York School, the politicised disruptions and syntactic disarray of Language poets, the surreal turns and openness of Black Mountain poets, and the political chant-mesmerism of the Beats. Gizzi's poems reverberate with these lineages while imbued with contemporary thinking and work: "The most forgotten history / is often the best" ('The Outernationale'). When viewed all together his poems display a unique and necessary ecological vision. Gizzi's project feels ecocentric, or Anthropocenic, almost by accident. Without an agenda for wilderness or the 'natural' world, there is in his poems an interesting corruption of what we see as 'nature': trees have a "superlative nature" in 'Every Day I Want to Fly My Kite', the world is "handmade" ('Fragment'), "Birdsong and daybreak" are the same "at the root" ('Tradition & the Invisible Talent'). There is a powerful self-reflexivity towards how a poet may utilise the external (natural) world, which gives the project of his poems this political, but quietly so, eco-conscious thread, and powers the more personal project of how we relay and relate the internal to the external.

When I think about what I want to read and write in a time of uncertainty, it is always poetry. I lean most to poetry because the poems I like most, those like Gizzi's, buck and kink at the idea of a linear narrative, of certainty in existence. I take solace in these structures of disrupture; they force a reader to comprehend logic outside of the logics we live in (as comfort) day to day. Disruption *is* kind of normality, and this feels more than ever so now. The global pandemic has meant any idea our civilisation had of a narrative, of a continuous or expected life, has been blasted from what was planned. Gizzi's poems, in their generosity of form and tone, in their scope, in their project dedicated to the sacred necessity of speaking human emotion (love, grief, pain and joy), and their contemporary and relatable demotic, are poems to be read now. In its newness and knowledge, his work is a gift to poetics, but it is also a human solace, especially when we think back to the words of 'Speech Acts for a Dying World' (and even that title gives serious attention to the importance of human communication and connection, through art and elsewhere):

> I thought I was done
> with time, its theatricality,
> glamour, and guff
>
> gusting cloud, I see you,
> I become you
> In my solitary thinging,
> here in partial light.

His vision is detailed, with its intense focus and exploration of the minutiae, and his language is like talking to your most erudite, brilliantly thoughtful and emotionally intelligent friend, but his scope is epic, and it is in these tensions that he calls in the world with such precision.

Rachael Allen is the author of Kingdomland *(Faber, 2019) and Poetry Editor at* Granta.

CONTRIBUTORS

Akpa Arinzechukwu is a Nigerian writer, photographer, and social activist for queer rights • **Fiona Benson**'s latest collection is *Vertigo & Ghost* (Cape, 2019) • **Susie Campbell** is studying for PhD at Oxford Brookes University. Her latest pamphlet is *Tenter* (Guillemot, 2020) • **Rachel Dbeis** is a trainee surgeon and literary translator from Beirut. She runs The Lesbanese Cook, which explores civil rights and sexuality in the Middle East through food • **Samar Diab** is a prolific Arabic poet and artist, author of *Hunāka 'irāk fī al-khārij* (2010) and *Mathaf al-ashyā' wa-al-kā'ināt* (2013) • **Kit Fan**'s *As Slow As Possible* was a PBS Recommendation. *Diamond Hill*, his debut novel, will be published in 2021 • **Jane Feaver** is a novelist and short-story writer based in south-west England • **Leontia Flynn**'s latest collection is *The Radio* (Picador, 2017) • **Eve Grubin** is the author of *Morning Prayer* (Sheep Meadow, 2006) • **Hasti C.** is a British-Iranian poet and screenwriter. She hosts FRESH LIP, a monthly open-mic in Peckham, south-east London • **Kaleem Hawa**'s debut poetry collection, *She Thinks She's the Passionate One* (2020), won the *White Review* Poet's Prize • **Eleanor Hooker**'s third poetry collection is due for publication 2021. She is a helm and Press Officer for Lough Derg RNLI Lifeboat • **Fawzia Muradali Kane** is an architect and poet, born in Trinidad and Tobago and author of *Tantie Diablesse* (Waterloo, 2011) and *Houses of the Dead* (Thamesis, 2014) • **Luke Kennard** is a poet and novelist who lives in Birmingham • **Ariel Klein** writes poetry and is working towards a PhD in cognitive science and language • **Tim Liardet** is the author of ten poetry collections and Professor of Poetry at Bath Spa University • **Fran Lock** is the author of seven poetry collections and numerous chapbooks, most recently *Contains Mild Peril* (Out-Spoken Press, 2019) • **John McCullough**'s latest collection, *Reckless Paper Birds* (Penned in the Margins) won the 2020 Hawthornden Prize • **Hugh McMillan**'s latest collections are *Heliopolis* and *The Conversation of Sheep*, both published by Luath in 2018 • **Lucy Mercer**'s poems have been widely published. She was awarded the inaugural *White Review* Poet's Prize • **Mary Meriam** co-founded Headmistress Press and edits the *Lavender Review: Lesbian Poetry and Art*. Her latest collection is *My Girl's Green Jacket* (2018) • **Valzhyna Mort** writes in Belarusian and English. Her latest book, *Music for the Dead and Resurrected*, is forthcoming from FSG • **Gboyega Odubanjo**'s pamphlet, *While I Yet Live*, was published by Bad Betty Press in 2019 • **Rainie Oet** is the author of *Porcupine in Freefall* (Bright Hill, 2019), *Inside Ball Lightning* (SEMO, 2020), and *Glorious Veils of Diane* (Carnegie Mellon, 2021) • **Kimberly Reyes** is a poet and essayist and the author of *Running to Stand Still* and *Life During Wartime* •• **Tommy Sissons** is a poet, political writer, educator, and the literary editor of *GRASS Magazine* • **Katharine Towers** has published two poetry collections with Picador and a third is forthcoming in 2021 • **Nerys Williams** is an Associate Professor in Poetry and Poetics at University College Dublin and the author of two poetry collections.

Australian Poetry

Australian Poetry, established to bring together state-based poetry collectives, publishes the country's national poetry journal, the *Australian Poetry Journal*. The Journal, published six-monthly, is guest-edited each issue by different voices, to ensure excellence and inclusivity. It also publishes insightful, curious articles. AP publishes an annual anthology, along with a digital volume showcasing U30s and emerging voices.

Based at Melbourne's The Wheeler Centre, alongside the UNESCO City of Literature Office, AP also partners with the major capital city literary festivals around the country each year, producing our own events. Annually, AP presents, commissions or publishes new works by 350+ Australian poets. We run local and international residencies and mentorships, and sit at record subscriptions.

To join AP as a subscriber, visit australianpoetry.org/support

Both print/digital and digital-only are available, from $30 per year. Or contact Jacinta Le Plastrier at ceo@australianpoetry.org

Already a subscriber but want to support AP further? Visit australianpoetry.org/support and donate there